DON'T GET ON THE PLANE

Also by Rene Jax

56 Sanchez
Altza Moorin and the green gill dragon
Altza Moorin and the cave of the black heart
Altza Moorin and the war of atonement
Kosher Conspiracy
The Soulful traveler
It's who we are, it's what we do.

DON'T GET ON THE PLANE
Copyright 2016 –
December 14, 2017
By Rene Jax

CONTACT EMAIL
renejaxiwritebooks@gmail.com

DON'T GET ON THE PLANE
By Rene Jax

Second Printing

Vs 1.0

December 14, 2017

Edited by Mark Fletcher

Cover jacket design by Amanda Mullins

FORWARD
BY
DAVID C.

I knew Jack for about a year. I've known Rene for forty more. They are one and the same. There was no hard and fast break; just a continuum. Jack was open, friendly, curious, personable. Faithful to a fault, and always willing to lend a helping hand. So too is Rene.

Forty years ago, when Jack didn't show up for a prearranged engagement, I got concerned (or perhaps I was pissed), and drove to his apartment. The shades were drawn. My knock went unanswered. I let myself in. Jack was huddled on the floor, in a corner, in the dark, weeping. When I asked him what was wrong, he revealed to me his lifelong struggle with his sexual identity. I'm not sure if I entirely believed him. He was a pretty regular guy. Tall, strong, a baritone who could do a spot-on Gregory Peck impression. He liked guns and martial arts and muscle cars. There was nothing overtly feminine about him. I had driven his wife, Jan, to college with me every day for a semester; Jack was using their vehicle and she needed a ride. She never mentioned anything. I didn't really understand Jack's decision to embark on this difficult journey, but his pain seemed real enough, so, as a friend, I accepted it. But now, after reading this manuscript, I think maybe I shouldn't have been so accepting. Maybe, as a friend, I should have intervened.

Instead, I was an enabler, albeit a passive one, just as so many others whom Jack sought out for help and direction, whether passive or active, whether friends or medical professionals, turned out to be.

Whether you are hesitating to board that plane, whether you've already booked that one way trip, or whether you're just a curious bystander wondering how we got to this place and time where "transitioning" is the cause du jour, read on. Rene Jax is an engaging writer with a fascinating, cautionary, tale to tell.

As for me and my dear friend, to paraphrase the common cliché uttered by newly minted in-laws, I didn't lose Jack, I gained Rene.

David C.
(Hollywood, California 2017)

Dedication

This book is dedicated to my personal therapist.

In the years I was in therapy with her, she saved my life on more than one occasion. She is also the person who signed the letter approving my sex change. She is a person I love and respect, who, when I told them I was writing this book, asked me why I would write a book that would discount and dismiss her entire life's work.

After much thought my answer is this.

Our time in therapy, and resulting years of friendship started me on the road that I now walk. I have traveled around the world with the skills and understanding that you helped, and sometimes forced me to learn. Now that I am at the finish line of this great journey, I have depth of perspective to see and to understand how you and your colleagues' past and present beliefs were formed. I understand now that it was those core beliefs about gender dysphoric patients, laid down over a century ago by Magnus Hirschfeld and Harry Benjamin led to the existing treatment options.

I could not have reached this level of understanding had you not helped me, and furthermore, had I not chosen to act upon yours and my other doctor's therapeutic beliefs. I think that we both understand how psychiatry and medicine are still in its infancy, and that those men and women who have fashioned our current understanding of gender and transsexualism were and are still simply trying to shed light and reason on our limited understanding of self and human identity.

Having said that, we now need to move beyond the notion that sex reassignment surgery is the necessary outcome for cross-sexual identity confusion. And it is long past time for the medical community to strip away the old definitions, and begin again to find a way through the labyrinth of cross-sex, identity-confused patients' mental illness with fresh eyes and determination.

History, (while chastising our predecessors for having taken too long to do so,) will I believe, praise us for finally bringing an end to this barbaric medical intervention and treatment. The patients whom we help to the other side of this maze without any chemical and surgical intervention will thank us.

I am forever grateful to you for helping me start this journey. This book is the natural finish line to that starting point.

Many deepest heartfelt thanks.

Rene Jax

TRANSSEXUALITY

"Sense of persistent identification with, and expression of, gendercoded behaviors not typically associated with one's sex at birth, and which were reducible neither to erotic gratification, nor psychopathological paraphilia, nor physiological disorder or malady."

Currah, Green, and Stryker (2008)

Preface

I caught the Southwest Airline out of San Jose Airport at seven in the morning. And after what seemed like a lifetime of traveling, a Greyhound bus I had caught in downtown Pueblo, Colorado dropped me off a few hundred feet from the Trinidad Motor Lodge at 2:45 a.m. It was November 12 1990, and the small farming town in Southern Colorado had its first snow two days before my arrival. Patches of frozen snow left over from the storm, covered parts of the parking lot. The cold ice undermined my footing as I walked up a slight incline toward the glowing "VACANCY" sign to check in. Minutes later, I stood in the bare-bones room and set down my small backpack on the bed. As tired as I was I could not force myself to sleep that night, and paced the floor of the small room for the next three hours. I wanted to run away. But I knew the Trinidad was the end of the road for me; I had nowhere to run to, no one to run to. As I wore a path in the old carpet, I wanted my life to have been different than it was, but it was not. I had grown up thinking of myself as a transsexual, a woman trapped in a man's body and the sex change surgery I was scheduled to have in two days· time was supposed to be what I had always wanted. So why was I *still*, at the finish line of a 35-year marathon, unable to sleep, and still questioning myself if a sex change was the right thing to do? How could I go into this life changing surgery and not be absolutely certain?

After six hours of pacing the floor, the sun had finally crept up over the Great Plains. Picking up my bag, I walked the few blocks to the First National Bank Building of Trinidad.

It was in this stone edifice where Dr. Stanley Biber had his office for the last thirty years. After a brief and cordial introduction, Dr. Biber spent all of four minutes giving me what he called "a medical examination." Satisfied that I would not die in surgery, (and before I knew it) I was walking down the metal stairs of the building on my way to the local hospital for my pre-surgical tests. Two days later, I was surgically castrated, and my penis used to create my new vagina.

How did I get here? Let's start at the beginning.

Everything I say is a lie.

This is the ultimate ethical, moral and philosophical conundrum.

Yet, this is my life's core philosophy.

It's how I've learned to survive in a world as a deviant, as a transsexual. By the time I was eight years old, I intuitively knew I had to lie about my feelings about myself to mother. I lied to my older brother and sister about why I liked to dress up in girls' clothing. During the few times my absentee father blew into town, I knew better than to tell him about my wanting to be a girl.

As I grew older, I began lying to my girlfriends and then eventually to my first wife, Janet. And while the central lie in my life revolved around my sexual identity confusion, its roots quickly spread across the entire landscape of who I was. Lying was my emotional defense mechanism and protected my deepest secret from all that would harm me. I lie, therefore I can't be hurt. With my decision to live full time as a woman in 1977, I forced myself to lie about my entire past, my family, my present, my sexuality, my gender, and my own body. I was on the defensive 24/7 and always at the ready to lie. The doctors and psychiatrist, who I paid to help me, encouraged my lies for the sake of the end result, i.e. passing as a woman in a society that feared and loathed deviants.

I have lied for the last half century about my sex and gender and it is time for me, and for you, to stop all the misdirection's, the power plays, the deceits, the subterfuge, and bring the lying about gender and transsexualism to a quick and final end.

I was born on Saturday, May 14 at 8:22 pm, a bouncing baby boy who weighted eight pounds, nine ounces, the third and last child to Loretta and Jack. I was the unplanned child to a couple whose marriage had been on the rooks for years. My father was by the time of my birth a confirmed alcoholic and my mother was a certifiable schizophrenic. At the time, I was conceived, it had already started to snow and my parent's relationship was the unsuspecting dinosaurs facing a certain extinction. Within four years of being born, my father had flown the coup, and my mother had fallen into the terminal purgatory of her mental illness. Neither of them ever came back from their self-imposed exiles, and I was immediately thrown into the role of being a parent to my ill mother and adult protector to my own child self. The Denver Public Library would soon become my personal sanctuary where I spent every possible moment trying to figure out my strange desires and feelings. I spent my youth reading through thick

19

medical books for answers to why I felt like I was a girl inside. Then one day I found a new book (1966) by Dr. Benjamin and found a label that would follow me for my lifetime…"Transsexual".

Eureka! I now had a reason for my madness. I now had a label that explained everything. I was a TRANSSEXUAL. Benjamin's book explained that I was "actually" a woman trapped in a man's body. I was not alone; there were others just like me! His book outlined how futile it was for me to fight my urges and that the only cure for my pain and confusion was sex change surgery. His words gave me my first glimmer of hope that, if I could take some female hormones, and have a sex change, my life would finally be alright.

I had a label—hallelujah I had a label!

Thank you, modern medicine I'm a transsexual!

This label, curtesy of Harry Benjamin helped me to explain my world to myself. Soon there were other books and studies that I found in the library. The collective works of Hirschfeld, Benjamin, Green and Money, Kinsey, and Robert Stoller would soon act as a gender development map that would guide and influence my actions for next forty years of my life. It was these men's words and research that defined and shaped my thinking, and subsequently, my decisions and expectations of what was possible for me. They, combined with the therapeutic advice of three other doctors and therapists I saw in person over the next fifteen years moved me toward a singular goal of having sex reassignment surgery in 1990 at the age of thirty-five. I now have lived more than a half century and have researched the field of gender confusion. In addition, having lived on the outskirts of society for most of my life, I have known and met hundreds of other transsexuals and gender-confused individuals during this time. It has now been twenty-six years since I lay on a gurney in front of Dr. Stanley Biber, the doctor who performed my sex reassignment surgery. And based on this first-hand, empirical observation, I can assuredly tell you that *it was all for naught.*

There is an old saying: When a person takes the time to tell you the truth…Listen!

- My Sex Change Surgery did nothing
- It accomplished nothing
- It changed nothing
- It was a waste of time and money
- My life got worse, not better
- The surgery didn't solve anything.

Sex Reassignment Surgery is not what its name implies. It is sexual mutilation, plain and simple. It serves no purpose other than to complete the story arc that has been dreamed up by four doctors. These four doctors studied the condition, but did not research it. They responded to their patient's emotional conflicts by offering surgery and hormones, but not by getting down to the core of what caused the condition. Collectively they were happy to treat the symptoms of this disorder, but not the cause of the dis-ease. Since Magnus Hirschfeld performed the first known sex change on

Einer Wegener nearly a century ago, countless other doctors and therapists have followed in his footsteps and treated their patients who suffer from this aliment with the very same techniques and treatment option. Yet, sex reassignment surgery is nothing less than sexual mutilation butchery perpetuated on the unsuspecting and innocent. It is performed by doctors and psychiatrists whose toolsets to treat gender confusion are completely inadequate to the task. By encouraging transsexual patients to have a sex change, doctors willingly and knowingly abandoning them/us to a permanent state of mental illness, social deviance and despair. And if you are considering this surgery, let me caution you further: It is completely unnecessary.

It is a road you do not have to take to find inner peace.

This book looks at the men who created the diagnoses of transsexuality and gender confusion and how the failed generations of patients with this illness. I also help shed light on how we must break out of their diagnosis and walk back into our lives, into society as whole persons that can have fulfilling lives.

I assure you that I am not a religious fanatic, driven by any particular dogma. Nor am I a social justice warrior trying to use you to move my political agenda forward for the perfect genderless utopian world.

I am a man that in his old age, has seen the error of his ways. My only hope in writing this book is to help others from taking the same plane that led me here.

Introduction

The intention behind this book is to save your life. The only reason I write this is to assure gender confused people that they no longer have to live their lives as outcasts in the world. I write this so they will not have to live out their years isolated from the people they love, chased off by friends and family, or forced by incurable loneliness to put a gun to their head and end the torment of having "chosen" to live life as a transsexual.

This book strips the façade off the entire medical industry and weaponization of transsexualism, and LGBT backed forced social acceptance of people with this condition. By illuminating the path that led us all here, it allows the light of reason and logic to finally see the lies, the distortions, and the shortcomings of the men who have intentionally and unintentionally led us down this twisted self-destructive path toward Sex Reassignment Surgery.

While I was forced by my own ignorance in the matter to trust the professionals who claimed knowledge of my identity confusion, I did not have the years of experience and wisdom I do now, to break away from the frivolity, ridiculousness and insanity of this "medical" diagnosis and treatment. Now, nearly thirty years after having my sex change, I am reaching out to you in hopes of helping you avoid the travesty that is the diagnosis of Transsexuality.

I certainly don't consider myself a victim of my early gender confusion. But I do consider myself guilty in having played into the hands of a medical profession that is largely complacent in allowing their medical colleagues to ignore all reason, logic and basic medical ethics when it comes to the treatment of individuals they call transsexuals. The entire Western medical profession is guilty of medical malpractice on a systemic level for allowing this quackery and butchery to go on since the 1930s.

Over the last hundred years, five men have been responsible for defining and categorizing an entire class of mental illness. The mental illness we are speaking of is when a person believes that they are a member of the opposite sex, living in the wrong body. The doctors who developed treatment options over the years for this condition, did so blindly and without any legitimate medical research into the cause of the condition, and in many cases, without extensive medical and or psychiatric training. As we see with Dr. Magnus Hirschfeld, his surgery of Einer Wegener was the direct result of his own personal political agenda, and without having performed any of the necessary research leading up to such a complicated surgery, was responsible for the death of Wegener. It is he and men like him who have colored and slanted the rest of the medical profession's viewpoint on treatment options for the transsexual/gender-confused patient. This handful of men created their very own lexicon and treatment guidelines for gender dsyphoric individuals without any challenge or questioning of their methods by other doctors in the medical and psychoanalytical professions.

Because of the small minority of people suffering from this condition (0.03%) (a number considered by doctors too small to be a threat to society,) their treatment methods are left unchallenged by the medical profession as a whole. Further, the doctors who have entered this field have been allowed to experiment on tens of thousands of unsuspecting patients with massive doses of cross sex hormones, and radical surgeries that endangered their patient's lives. These experimental medical procedures have left their patients freaks of nature; neither male nor female, but living in a perpetual purgatory of sexual ambiguity. Left unchallenged and unchecked for the last 100 years, the idea of transsexual/gender dsyphoric or third-sex individuals has now blossomed into a social cult whereby any person who is so inclined or so confused as to their own sexual nature, can now remain in the comfort of sexual adolescence forever, and avoid taking on the responsibilities of an adult man or woman by merely claiming to feel "like they are trapped in the wrong body"

Even the US President Barak Obama has been bought into this falsehood without ever challenging the most simple and basic assumptions around the condition. He and his "advisors" have been unwilling to look into any medical or psychiatric research that runs contrary to this popular dogma. This uninformed president aggressively pushed acceptance of mentally ill patients onto the general population for the sake of political correctness. This book details how doctors and mental health therapists turned simple social identity confusion into a mental health condition they termed "untreatable". Armed with this label, they justified their own abandonment of the most basic tenet of the Hippocratic Oath:

"I will apply, for the benefit of the sick, all measures which are required, avoiding those twin traps of overtreatment and therapeutic nihilism"

In plotting the course on how the treatment and care for identity confused people came about these many years, we are able to take a fresh and unabashed look at the underlying issues and factors that help to cause the confusion "transsexuals" feel. In doing so, we can quickly break down when, where and by whom that logic and reason fell by the wayside. This alone will help you to rid yourself of century's worth of medical baggage that is now attached to this condition.

My fifty years of personal experience in this area will help you to see your situation clearly for the first time. And at the end of this book, you will see how to rid yourself of these worthless and destructive labels, and to forget all the nonsense and lies that these clinicians and charlatans have perpetuated upon all of us who have questioned our role in society. You will finally free yourself from the stigma of a medical diagnosis that simply does not exist. I am convinced that a century from now, future societies will view this last 100 years of treating the gender confused with hormones, plastic surgery, and genital mutilation as a nothing less than butchery and unnecessary medical experimentation.

CHAPTER ONE

<u>WHAT THIS BOOK IS ABOUT</u>

This book is an overview of the men who created Transsexualism and Gender Dysphoria, and how their definitions have led thousands of unsuspecting and innocent people into the abyss that their categorization created. This book is in response to the weaponization of gender confusion by leftists who care more about their agenda, then for the individuals who suffer from it.

I have laid out the format of the research chronologically, so as to make it simple for the average person to see the path by which we got to this point in time. By looking at this subject from a system's perspective, we are able to see the mistaken steps in the development and understanding of cross-gender identity and its related obsession. I have attempted to be fair to the men responsible for the current treatment options of cross-gender identity individuals. But I admit to a great deal of personal bias in the matter.

My personal belief in the concept of transsexualism ultimately led me to be surgically castrated through sex reassignment surgery (SRS) Twenty-six years later, that surgery has allowed me to review and challenge my own core beliefs on the subject. Subsequently I no longer am a disciple of the men and their opinions profiled in this book. I honestly don't believe I have regrets in the matter. I could have only taken the road I was standing on, and now stand on an entirely new road in a different part of the world. It is with this new perspective that I view the medical and psychiatric treatment for people like myself.

I am now sixty-one years old, and sincerely thought that my days of inquiry and caring about gender and transsexualism were long past. Believing I am at the end game of my life, I had resigned myself to the outcome of my decisions, good or bad. I fully understand that, unlike many of the first-person video games I love so dearly, there is no re-spawning that would allow me to redo this move, or that bad…first step. With maturity comes the resignation to the choices I've made. Over these last few years, I've simply wanted to keep my head down, continue working a decent job as long as I am physically able, and avoid pissing off my current boss … to that end, "God please let me live indoors and eat daily." I don't think that is asking for much. But then I came to a new junction in my end game about two years back.

I was housesitting for a friend in the Denver area, and searching online for an Apple technician to help with a question I had. As with most unlikely events, I discovered a friend whom I lost track of nearly 25 years previously. "Karen" was my dearest friend back in the late 1980s, and helped me get through my sex change. I couldn't have done it without her. Not long after my surgery, Karen, who was also a male-to-female transsexual, had her surgery, and I did everything I could to return her friendship. But somehow, and I'm certain you understand these things, we lost track of one another. She took her road and I took mine. But then, after nearly three decades, I found her online. There I was, sitting across from Karen at lunch and it brought up all of the big issues from so long ago. We had both grown old. Our once blond hair had turned white in the process of living out our dreams. In my lifetime, I have known hundreds of people that have suffered from gender identify confusion. Many of these people had serious mental illness issues other than gender confusion. But not Karen—she was the most mentally and emotionally solid of all the transies I have ever known. And in the course of our lunch together in Denver, the evitable topic came up. She made an interesting observation: She said that when she was living as a man, her outside life was calm and her inside (mental) life was chaotic. Now, thirty years after her sex change, her inside life was calm, but her outside life has been in chaos. Her words kept percolating in my mind as I drove away from our visit . They echoed my own personal experience, prior to having SRS.

"My mental life was filled with anguish." This is a common complaint from people diagnosed with gender confusion. But after the surgery that constant state of agitation slowly rescinded, and I was successful in tamping down any lingering doubts about my decision, until my lunch with Karen. Her words forced me to take a deep, retrospective analysis of my life as it relates to gender, and my subsequent decisions to commit myself fully to this path. In the two years hence, I have re-read all of the original medical textbooks, analysis, and research that the pioneers in the field have produced over the last one hundred and thirty years. This re-examination of the theoretical foundations for transsexualism and gender dysphoria, combined with a half century of empirical life experience, has led me to the fully unvarnished opinion that we have been on the wrong path

In order for you to understand why, you must first understand the men who helped guide the medical and psychiatric profession to this point, and how their lives were shaped. Part One of this book looks at the most significant individual contributors in the field, and examines their particular donation to our current beliefs. Part Two explores the ethical and moral dilemmas surrounding the current treatment options for people diagnosed as transsexuals, and shows just how insane the treatment options are. Also I identify where the real problem lies, at what stage it develops in childhood, and how modern-day psychiatry gave up finding the root cause of the condition. I show individuals where to search for answers and how to learn to live with their identity confusion.

For the sake of balance in this book, I need to make it absolutely clear, that I do NOT believe in:

- TRANSSEXUALISM
- CORE GENDER IDENTY
- INDIVIDUALS HAVING A GENDER
- GENDER DYSPHORIA
- GENDER AS A FLUID STATE OF IDENTITY

I will break down where and how these concepts came into being and how they have contributed to the misunderstanding of cross-sex identity confusion (CSIC). No, I am NOT politically correct. I believe and will explain in this book how gender dysphoria and its related phases is a personality disorder that qualifies as a mental illness.

To begin with, there is a growing push by advocates of transsexual acceptance in the United States to normalize the condition throughout the country. It has even reached the President of the United States. He recently supported a campaign to force the entire country into accommodating gender-confused individuals in schools and public places. I, as a transsexual, should be fully supportive of this move. But I am assuredly not! As of this date, there has only been two scientifically-based research projects on the viability of a transsexual lifestyle and SRS. The first of these was researched by Dr. Jon Meyer of John Hopkins University and is now over 35 years old. The second, done recently in Sweden mirrors the results of Dr. Meyer's results. Both research shows that about 44% of all people who have SRS attempt suicide. This is a rate nearly 65% higher than the entire general population. Transsexual suicide rates make dentist suicide rates look like rant amateurs. It was this study of the John Hopkins Medical Schools own post-surgical patients that led that famed hospital to discontinue offering SRS. When this study came out in the late 1970s, many providers of the surgery assailed it as biased, but never did they question their own beliefs that by physically mutilating a person would "fix" a patient whose condition is entirely mental in nature. This is akin to the long outdated practice of performing CPR on patients who have suffered myocardial infarct. What you are never told when about those CPR classes offered by the American Red Cross is that they are never going to bring your dear aunt back from the dead. You were simply trying to push a tiny bit of oxygenated blood through her veins until the ambulance arrived and hopefully get her to the hospital before she became braindead. Since the majority of heart attacks are mechanical/chemical failures of the heart itself, you could bounce up and down on dear old Aunt Mary's chest until you were blue in the face, but it wouldn't help.

In my youth, I worked at a Colorado hospital on a Cardiac Arrest Team. This team would respond en masse anytime a patient would arrest. We had all the latest tools and drugs right at our fingertips. Yet even with those tools, our internal research showed that the survival rate for patients who "coded" was lower than

4%. Everyone on the team knew that number, yet every time the alarm sounded, we would rush our crash carts to the patient's bed and do our best dance to try to save someone that we knew in our hearts never had a snowball's chance in hell of coming from death's door. SRS is exactly the same situation: It's using plastic surgery to treat emotional problems.

The same is true for the current sad state of transsexual therapy options. Massive doses of hormones, and plastic surgery _are not_ what people suffering from CSIC need. Nor does signing a letter stating that the patient has met the standard for being a transsexual, allowing them to run off to Thailand or Casablanca or Trinidad or where ever, to have a sex change make any sense. Here is a very simple question for those medical practitioners reading this:

Is the transsexual patient basically confused /conflicted about themselves, and their role in society as a man or woman?

The recognized goal of all psychotherapeutic analysis is to:

1) To know yourself better.

2) Alleviate emotional pain or confusion.

3) Assist the patient in developing a more complete understanding of their psychological issues.

4) Establish more effective coping mechanisms.

5) Foster a more accurate understanding of a patient's past and what they want for their future.*

Therefore, if the above goals for the entire field of psychiatry are reasonable and logical, then why would a treatment plan for this solitary, particular class of patients ever include options such as cross-sex hormones, plastic surgery, breast augmentation or reduction, hysterectomies, facial electrolysis, living in the role of the opposite sex, legally changing their name to one of the opposite sex, and surgical castration and mutilation? All of the above treatment options have one thing in common: they force the patient out of harmony with their families, society, workplaces, schools, and lovers, further alienating them from the love and support they are seeking. If a key foundational goal of therapy is to "alleviate emotional pain or confusion," then why on God's green earth would you offer/allow/permit options that promote more pain and confusion? I will tell you all right now, that the answer is not to force transsexual bathroom use on the general public, nor to force businesses to hire people who are confused about their social roles.

The answer is certainly not to attempt to legally mandate or legislate acceptance of transsexuals within society. ARE YOU F**KING KIDDING ME?

Let's dig into this wound a little bit, shall we? Here you have an individual who is not feeling okay about his or her role in society. Yet some of you actually want to force employers to hire people who are having problems coping in society? Nope, there's no pressure there for the transsexual to fit in, nope, not at all! I know what will help the confused person fit in—let's shine a massive spotlight on these individuals through legislative action and by mandating that everyone in the workplace accept them in spite of opinions and religious viewpoints that conflict with that legislation. Let's try forcing everyone in society to think about the transsexual in the same in way their sympathetic gay friends and therapist does. Let's force transsexuals into workplaces, into schools, and into public bathrooms and throughout society. How do some of you suggest that is this going to help make us fit into the rest of society any better? How is this approach ultimately going to help the CSIC patient resolve their confusion and loneliness any better by having all of society resent them?

   This is certainly not a civil rights issue, as defined by the US Attorney General.

It is nothing more than an unabashed attempt at social engineering. How can any of these legal maneuvers help people with a mental illness work through their emotional issues, when every action and word they utter is now under a gigantic social microscope, tweeted and Facebooked for the entire world to see, twenty-four hours a day? How is this approach supposed to allow the sexually confused person fit into society and social structures?

It isn't.

Let me tell you a little story. In 1978 I was living in San Francisco's gay community, called the Castro. I had been doing a lot of work in the community and wanted to take it to the next level. I was in my third year on female hormones and living as a woman, though I still had male anatomy. I passed pretty well for what I had to work with, and had a nice little life going for myself in the gay ghetto that was the Castro back then. I had lots of friends, was fucking like a little rabbit most weekends, went to a lot of bars and clubs on days off, and was generally a happy little TS and living my life "as" a woman. Somehow, I found out there was an auxiliary police force called San Francisco Patrol Special Police, and they were looking for a person to patrol the Castro. It didn't have the same rules for hiring as the "regular" department, and after some research on my part, I met the officer in charge of the district. Jack Menn was Patrol Special Officer in charge of the Castro best. He was a large, old-school cop with big hands and an even bigger laugh. I came out to him, told him my entire story, and without hesitation, and much to his credit as a human, he offered me the job. At first, the San Francisco Police Chief would have none of it. After he received my application, he told me to my face and in NO UNCERTAN WORDS, that it would be a cold day in hell before the likes of me got sworn in as a police officer. Remember this was 1979 and the world of law enforcement was still fighting against women and blacks joining their ranks. So I, being full of piss and vinegar, fought and fought and fought the department and spent every penny I made as a security guard on lawyers to assist in my battle to be hired by Jack Menn. Finally, on June 8, 1980, the San Francisco Police department having run out of all legal options, reluctantly swore me in as the world's first transsexual police officer. Now that should have been the last of it my troubles but it wasn't. It was only round one of a daily battle with the regular police officers, that I worked alongside every hour of the day. For the next two years my life was a living hell. The police management were forced to swear me in, but the rank and file would have none of it, and every day as I worked Castro street in uniform, regular police officers verbally threatened me, vandalize my car on a routine bases, and often would put my life at risk by not backing me up when I was in tight spots with the bad guys. I was thankfully stupid enough to have thick skin going into it, but after 700 days of this shit, it wore me down to nothing. The final straw came when I went to the aid of a woman being attacked up in the Diamond Heights apartment complex. I was sitting in my car doing some paperwork when I saw a man break into an apartment building. I used my police radio to call it in, and then stupid me, went after the guy. By the time I made it into the building, he had broken down the woman's door and was attempting to rape her. Long story short, the assailant was on PCP and kicked the living shit out of me. Then he smiled, and walked calmly back to his car without a word. My radio was broken, my flashlight was broken and my back was nearly snapped in two. I was also bleeding from a dozen cuts and lacerations. The rape victim was in shock from her ordeal, and slammed the door on me while I lay on the hallway floor bleeding. By the time I stumbled outside, a regular black and white police unit arrived in response to my earlier call. When the police officer at the wheel saw it was me, their "least favorite faggot in the world," he drove off without offering any help. That was my last night in uniform. It took me nearly six months to recover from my injuries. The point of all this sad tale is that legislation can't make people tolerate or even like you. Even the Supreme Court can't force people to come around. Some of you might argue the success of racial integration laws. The reason that integration in America went relatively smoothly in 1972 was that the majority of American's weren't overly prejudiced toward other races. Everyone I knew had grown up with blacks, Irish, and Hispanics. When I was growing up in the late 1950s, Denver also had a large Chinese population, and my mother had many Asian friends. We were not rich people and most of us were all working-class families. The reason there is so much backlash today in 2017 around gays and transsexual rights is not from people hating queers and transies. Even my most red-neck friend knows of gay people among his family or neighbors.

It is from these forced agenda to social engineer a minority lifestyle into acceptance in the 99% of the population.

I do not think for a moment that any other person should go through what I did. This is not about civil rights and the Woolworth's lunch counter in 1961. What I am talking about is repulsion of our feeble attempts to cross live at the deepest and most biological level on the part of people. We are not, as Fritz Perls stated: "pushing the river" when one sex attempts to masquerade as the other. What we are attempting to do is on the scale of re-engineering the entire flow and nature of the human race. And hear me when I say from experience, *it will never work.* Transsexuals aren't just going against social "norms" we are going against human DNA.

All of humanity since our earliest ancestor nearly two million years ago, is to find a suitable mate to breed with. People know in their DNA genes what is male and what is a female, this is crucial for the survival of our species. We have to have this part and partial of what we are in order to keep our organism mating and reproducing. Even the best transsexual can't hide from this innate knowledge that even the most low brow redneck understands.

Nor do I advise people who are suffering from this condition to continue to obsess with the "what if I lived in the opposite sex" fantasy. This is unhealthy in the extreme and leads people suffering from this condition to think that there is solution, a magic pill outside of themselves that will fix their feelings and confusion.

All of the transsexuals I have known over the last forty years who have had the surgery, have one little secret that we never tell any other living person. It is believed that this secret, if ever spoken aloud, will instantly kill the person uttering it. It is a secret so vile that speaking it becomes a curse. It is the most awful and terrible truth the world has ever known. But for the sake of being honest with you, I shall share it with you again.

"SEX REASSIGNMENT SURGERY IS WORTHLESS, IT IS COMPLETELY AND UTTERLY FALSE A PREMISE. IT IS A WASTE OF YOUR HARD-EARNED MONEY. NONE OF THE CONFUSION AND EMOTIONAL PAIN YOU ARE NOW GOING THROUGH WILL CHANGE AS A RESULT OF BEING SEX REASSIGNMENT SURGERY. AFTER THE DUST SETTLES FROM THE SURGERY, YOU WILL STILL HAVE THE SAME ISSUES AND FEELINGS OF CONFUSION THAT YOU DID BEFORE BUT AFTERWARD WILL BE MORE OF AN OUTCAST THAN EVER BEFORE"

Having SRS does *nothing* to change or alleviate cross-sexual confusion. NOTHING! It does nothing to help bring emotional peace to your life. It solves nothing. The only thing having SRS does is to permanently close the door of reasonable options in a person's life that could help fix the central problem. That's it. On the other side of surgery is just more confusion of who you are, regardless of what is or is not between your legs. On the other side of SRS is more social rejection, more nasty looks from strangers, more loneliness. Unless you eliminate the personality disorder behind being a transsexual, you will forever remain confused about your identity.

Not A, and not B, just a f**ked-up C. Just like before the surgery.

Further, SRS further alienates a person from their family and friends. It removes the "transsexual" from playing any normal role in society from that point forward and fully eliminates the possibility of that person ever having any normal functional relationship. As I've stated previously, I have known hundreds of transsexuals and have never, ever met one that had a socially functional relationship post-surgically. My friend Karen is the closest person I know to being a functioning TS. But she was a highly functional person before she started living full-time as a woman.

The primary reason for this is that in our world, and the entire history of our species, there have only been two sexes. Two sexes, not one sex, not three, and not seven. Not male, once was female, or female, once was male. And this basic fact is deep in our DNA, influencing how we all think and act and behave. Our need to procreate, the cornerstone of who and what we are as a species, is guided by this drive. The two-million year history of our species is built upon this single fact, and when a person of one sex attempts to mimic the attributes of the other, all of the members (both male and female) of our species know on some diabolically-deep biological level that there is something not right about individual C. I know I am repeating myself several times here, but once you understand this core aspect of humanity as an organism, you will see the futility of all plastic surgery in the matter.

Speaking from experience, no matter how great you or I pass in public, people, and ironically sometimes the dumbest of people, instantly figure it out. Not A, and not B. And it's not just society that the transsexual has to think about. After the SRS, every day that the TS person wakes up, _they_ know they are not A and not B, but C. They know they have to take hormones, they know they have to spend more time working on the façade of being A or B than does every other person.

Twenty-seven years after my SRS, I wake up and immediately have to ensure that I fit into society. Being me, as I present myself, is not a natural state of being. And unlike the rest of this world, I just can't wake up and be Rene Jax, the woman. I have had the privilege of living and working around the world. I have lived in several Muslim countries where I could suffer greatly if people read me as male. So every day I am still dealing with my transsexualism and gender confusion, like I was when I was ten years old. The magnitude and texture of the issues change as I've grown older, but having had sex reassignment surgery hasn't eliminated any of the underlying issues in my life. It hasn't made life easier; it has only eliminated my options for solving it once and for all.

This book helps to redefine and reposition the starting point for people who are confused about their sexual identity. CSIC is specific to the condition and helps us to re-orient the discussion of therapy and treatment options from a new beginning.

It really isn't my desire to place blame on the feet of medical professionals. But I confess that sometimes I feel unbridled rage at the machine that is medical science. This rage has come out at the most unexpected moments while writing this work. After an especially difficult realization I may have while writing, I will lie down at night and yell at the universe over the injustice of it all. But when you find me sitting on my high horse of indignation and railing against the immorality and unethical treatment we as a class of patients have received, *I am equally at fault. I did not question the doctors' base assumptions or logic deeply enough when I was young.* I did not work hard enough to thoroughly understand their reasoning before I made the ultimate decision to have my SRS. *Like Hirschfeld and Benjamin before me, it was my own impatience, mental laziness and personal pain that led me to take that final step towards accepting sexual surgical mutilation as a real option for my identity confusion.*

I would love to think that the rationale outlined in this book as treatment options for individuals suffering with gender identity disorder is the ultimate guide to treatment. But then I would certainly join the ranks of those men I have faulted for doing the same thing. So, I suggest that this is *NOT THE DEFINITIVE WORK* on the subject. Please consider this only as a new starting place in the re-exploration and the re-examination of CSIC and its treatment options.

And be fully aware, the real responsibility for a successful therapeutic outcome for CSIC is not the doctors, therapists, psychiatrists, nor psychologists who treat these patients. It rests solely with the individual suffering from it and their family. It is the individual and their family members that must do all of the heavy lifting. It is the individual who must break down their own insanity and rigid viewpoint of their place in society as a male or female, and ultimately fix what was broken inside of them in the past. This is the greatest challenge ever asked of you.

I encourage each of you challenged by this condition, or treating patients with this condition, to not take the easy way out. If you are a medical professional, I beg you to not to sign a letter for any patient to have a sex change, because once you do, it will not wipe away your responsibility for the mental laziness in treating these patients. If you suffer from this condition, I appeal to the last reasonable brain cell left in you, don't be the person pacing back and forth in their hotel room the night before a sex change. Don't be the person trying to decide in a cold, lonely hotel room which is the lesser evil of the options you have.

By choosing not to live in the opposi[ ] you choose life in the community of man. Y[ ] having options in your life. You choose love.

First year of cross living

CHAPTER TWO

A ROAD TO HELL, PAVED WITH GOOD INTENTIONS.

This picture is of flowers I received from my best friend, and former lover after my sex change surgery in Trinidad, Colorado in 1990.

I am reminded of a saying in the construction trade: "You can't cheat a cheat." The Cheat they are referring to is work that is less than plumb, properly squared, or imperfect. In order to fix one tradesman's poor workmanship, the next has to "cheat" a little around the edges. So as the story goes, the guy who surveyed the property lines and foundation was in a bit of a hurry, and thus was a little off on setting the level of the rebar as it sat in the ground. So then the concrete guy comes in and seeing how the survey is off level, "cheats" a little to try to correct the first guy's work. Then the framers come in and see how the concrete slab is not quite level. They in turn "cheat" on the plumb of the wall frames. Then the sheetrock guys see how the framers plumb was off, and "cheat" on installing their sheetrock. Finally the door and window tradesmen come in, and the entire house is out of plumb. With all the walls at screwy angles, they can't begin to put in the doors and windows. Hence, "you can't cheat a cheat."

When looking at the evolution of treatment for CSIC over the last 150 years, this old expression about cheating keeps coming to mind. Every single person who has delved into the condition has left an indelible "cheat" for the next person to deal with. Contemporary doctors are then left to face the problem of trying to "square" their work within the treatment options defined by their earlier predecessors. A century later, the medical and psychiatric perspectives are now completely askew from their collective slanted "cheats" on the subject. And whilst many other lines of scientific research, such as immunology, have successfully built layer upon layer on the failure and achievements of previous analysis, research and experimentation, cross-sex identity confusion treatment and therapy has not. It remains seated firmly in its original interpretation and medical treatment performed by Hirschfeld and Benjamin and Money.

Let's start by examining the history of cross-sex identified individuals.

Any casual search of the internet will turn up a small group of people, who, prior to 1900, were born one sex, and for various reasons (most of them undocumented) adopted the persona and lifestyle of the opposite sex. Perhaps the most famous is Joan of Arc. She was born in 1412, and while still in her teens began dressing in male clothing. Other women who have dressed and lived in the role of men include Albert Cashier, Peter Hagby, and James Berry. It is well documented that the Roman Caesar Nero was known to dress in women's clothes, giving poetry recitals and perform as a female in plays. Whether or not this was from our condition or just weirdness on his part is unknown. There are many oral accounts of Native Americans who were called Berdaches. These were typically males who lived in the role of females. In India, there is a third sex of men living and dressing the role of women, called Hijira, the Hindi word for "migration."

It is important for us to not assume that all of these historical accounts were caused by cross-sex identity confusion and ideation. Two accounts of women living as men and joining the army were the result of poverty, caused by their husbands going to war. Attempting to label all cross-sex lifestyles from the past as "transsexuality" is foolish. Just as it would be in the present to make a simple generalization about the following people:

- A homosexual drag queen who dresses as Marilyn Monroe in a drag show for money.
- A heterosexual transvestite who likes to dress as a French Maid for sex with his wife.

- A woman who joins the Union Army as a man, after her husband abandons her to join himself.
- A Thai "lady-boy," who is hetroexual, but makes a living performing sex while dressed as a girl.

All three are cross dress in the opposite role, but all approach cross dressing from completely different reasons and perspective's.

With the exceptions noted here, there are very few reliable historical accounts around cross-sex identity confusion until the mid-1880s. This new repository of information about human sexuality was a direct result of the growth and modernization of mechanical printing, popular medicine, and its new bouncing baby, psychiatry.

It was with the sudden boom of new medical schools in Europe and the United States in the early 1880s, that a new understanding of the human condition slowly began to develop. With the growth of the medical profession as a trade came an increased willingness to discuss what was once thought private, as well as an awareness of human sexuality and deviant behavior. This wasn't to say that deviant behavior hadn't been part of human history up until that time, but rather that written history was under the control of three major religions. There is no reason to expect the clergy to document the majority of human frailties and sexual deviations as part of their documentation. Perhaps there is actually a collection buried deep inside the cavernous Vatican City archives. Regardless of any hidden textbooks the majority of people in the ancient world were illiterate. Even today it is estimated that nearly thirty-five percent of the world is illiterate. So it is not surprising that the most basic answers to questions about human sexuality where not publicly recorded until the growth of the Western-European medical profession. With the introduction of "trained" doctors moving out into communities came a deeper personal and professional understanding of people's sexuality, based on their interactions with patients. For the first time in history, cases of patients with interesting conditions and diagnoses were routinely disseminated and regularly published. Though there were many earlier medical publications, it was not until the *New England Journal of Medicine* began publication in 1812 that medical science was available to the average doctor and lay person. With this repository of knowledge came more awareness of people who were living, or wanting to live, as the opposite sex.

The doctors who contributed to the current medical thinking about cross-sex identity confusion were, I believe, all acting in relative good faith when they first prescribed their various treatments. I can't believe otherwise. For the last century, one doctor after another has built their theories about transsexuality and gender dysphoria treatment upon the very immature framework that modern medicine actually is. And their good intentions to help their patients have ultimately led us to a dead end.

But let's look at a parallel situation to SRS. Throughout the world, women's activist groups have emerged to challenge the historic practice of female genital mutilation (FGM), a practice dating back thousands of years, and meant to de-sex female children. By all conservative accounts, there are over 300 million women alive today who have been victims to this practice. The medical profession in over 100 countries is attempting to rid the world of this butchery. Yet, that same medical profession says nothing when a doctor signs a form approving a female to male transsexual patient to have her breasts, uterus and ovaries removed.

Why?

Because one is considered standard accepted treatment by the medical profession, whereby the patient is told of the risks and post-operative issues, and has given their consent, while this isn't the case with FGM. I personally find the moral abyss between the two disturbing. In proceeding chapters, I explore this dichotomy to a much greater degree. I have great discomfort with the laxity with which the medical profession has willingly drawn this arbitrary line. They do so as to favor poorly researched treatment and understanding in the arena. My greater issue with sex re-assignment surgery as a "viable" treatment option is the fact that it is simply meant to solve the underlining issues in cross-sex identified patients. Doctors do so because they are unable to make inroads into lessening, modifying, and or resolving their patient's confusion. If "giving up" on incurable patients weren't such a common practice in the mental health field, is would normally be considered medical malpractice. It should be a criminal act for a doctor to permit a patient to permanently mutilate their body based on pathological aspects of a mental illness. Yet every day of the year, there is a person having SRS. And in every single patient's file is a letter from a doctor stating that this patient has met the standards of care guidelines. In addition to releasing the surgeon from liability, it relieves the treating psychiatrist from legal, moral, and ethical claims.

The patient has signed a consent form.

The patient is informed of the procedure.

The patient has been told of the risks.

The patient understands that medical science is not a guarantee of results.

So, I guess we are all good then…RIGHT? Our transsexual patient signed a form releasing all doctors from liability. CHECK!

Our crazy tranny patient was told all about how the procedure is done. CHECK! Our kindly surgeon sat on the patient's bedside and explained all the terrible possible complications from the sex change. ANOTHER CHECK!

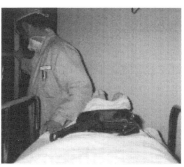

On my way into SRS surgery

And like all good hospital medical procedures, and to just cover all possible legal bases, the patient is told and must sign off to the fact that NO ONE, not the doctors, not the lawyers, not the best mind in the hospital can determine what the real and final outcome of any surgery or procedure is really going to be.

ANOTHER CHECK!

And with those four CHECKS in place, the "well-informed" transsexual patient lays on a gurney and is wheeled into a cold surgical suite, where they hope the end of their emotional pain will end.

I have been that person. When I woke up from my surgery the next day, I had a beautiful bouquet of flowers from my therapist next to my bed. There is a picture of them at the start of this chapter.

What the medical release forms don't say, and what the letter from my kind therapist didn't go openly state is that I was out of options in my life. I had been in therapy for fifteen-years with various doctors and counselors each trying unsuccessfully to deal with my cross-sex identity confusion. No traditional approach worked, and no amount of talking about my childhood, (using Freud's model of psychoanalysis) did any good to rid myself of the feelings that I was a girl trapped in a boy's body. After nearly two decades, I still loved dressing up in women's clothes. I craved putting on makeup and women's undergarments, feeling they were what I should be wearing, not suits and ties. I had wanted to live full-time as a woman since I was about ten years old. After years of talking about every nuance of my gender issues in therapy, I was committed to living my life as a woman and escape the pain I felt as a man.

What my therapist didn't and couldn't tell me was that I would lose my family's love, that I would be raped by potential lovers, that I would lose the love and support of future lovers…and this would go on for the balance of my life. She could not have foreseen the fact that I would lose countless jobs regardless of how competent I was, or how hard I worked. She could not foretell the fact that I would be routinely attacked by strangers while I walked down the street or was shopping in stores simply for my being different. What none of the people who had gone before me knew was:

Sex reassignment surgery was the doctors' and therapists' way of saying (to themselves) that they were giving up <u>all</u> hope of ever helping me fix my cross-sex identity confusion, and that their tools didn't work to fix this condition.

Sex reassignment surgery (SRS) is the last trick up doctor's sleeves to help chronically suffering patients. I believe every doctor knows that SRS is the last resort for their destitute, mentally ill patients with this disorder. If there is a doctor that does not believe it, I'm sure they are suffering from the same politically correct delusions as many of their PC activist patients. Few people who present themselves with cross-sex identity confusion (CSIC) are ever emotionally and financially stable enough to pay the exorbitant medical costs for the surgery. That fact alone reduces the need to write letters for 85% of their patients. As is often the case with of patients in this group, most have various aspects of mental illness that are blended with and masked by CSIC. Out of the remaining 15%, the majority in this group obsesses with living full-time in the opposite sex role, and may on various occasions, play around by doing it. Ultimately, they either don't have the coping skills for living a deviant lifestyle, or their personality disorder/mental illness is at the level of dysfunctionality that would drive them to live as the opposite sex and consider SRS.

Most problematic in the standard treatment approach is the fact that SRS is considered the ultimate outcome for "true" CSIC patients. This mindset was first established by Dr. Harry Benjamin in the late 1950s. It is now the accepted treatment option for CSIC. By getting on the plane to have the surgery, the person is committing themselves to living the balance of their lives on the fringes of a society that will never accept them. Why is it that full acceptance of a CSIC patient's birth sex and integration into society as a member of their sex, NOT the recognized and accepted long-term treatment plan? Why is this the one medical condition known to man that promotes the patient to mutilate themselves sexually?

Why is it that historical and contemporary treatments for CSIC patients _do not_ adhere to the same standards for _every other_ psychiatric patient? Why is it that, with all we've learned over the last seventy-five years, the minimal standards for treating people with mental illness are not followed? Conversely, the fact that CSIC patients are excluded from internationally recognized best psychiatric and medical practice standards, clearly places sex reassignment surgery firmly into the realm of

Nazi medical experimentation and not into the realm of contemporary medical treatments.

It is understandable though, when reading about the history of medicine, that despite recent advances in the treatment of all illness, many gaps in the understanding of physical and mental illness still exist. It was not that long ago that a good surgeon was a fast surgeon. But for doctors and psychiatrists who, in their treatment of CSIC patients are willing to give up all moral and ethical standards because of the lack of legitimate research, there are no excuses for abandoning ethical and morally acceptable standards of care.

By accepting the contemporary standards of care as inclusive of CSIC patients, rather than excluding of them, allows us to then we can take a fresh look at the overall pathology of the condition and possible treatment options with untarnished eyes and perspectives.

What I am proposing is a simple and sensible approach that will carry the medical profession and the patients they treat into the 21st century.

First day as a S.F. Patrol Special Police Officer

CHAPTER THREE

MENTAL ILLNESS THROUGH THE AGES

The Merriam Webster Dictionary defines mental illness as "medical conditions that are marked primarily by sufficient disorganization of personality, mind, or emotions to impair normal psychological functioning and cause marked distress or disability and that are typically associated with a disruption in normal thinking, feeling, mood, behavior, interpersonal interactions, or daily functioning."

Throughout the recorded history of our species there has been mention of people whose behavior falls within this definition. For all intents, it appears that mental illness is part and parcel of being human. People who sustain head injuries can develop mental problems, chemicals or lack thereof are known to change brain chemistry, and advanced age affects people's cognitive functioning. History has shown that exposure to war and violence has played a contributing factor to the sudden onset of mental illness in people. Over the centuries, we have learned that day-to-day stress impairs mental acuity and reaction time, and that poor choices in our mates can often create genetic flaws in our offspring. There appears to be just as many causes that affect and alter our mental functions as there are resultant conditions.

The start of recorded history dates back over 6 thousand years. While some historians debate the actual date of when that history begins, many point to the ancient Greeks as a tipping point for our recorded history. It was the Greeks who transformed the narrative of simply recording dates and events, and developed a true perspective on the people who lived. It was the Greeks who expanded recorded history into a retrospective analysis and discussion of ideas and concepts. And for the sake of our discussion, we will use that civilization as our starting point to look at the history of mental illness.

Records from that early time make mention of people who are mentally ill. Most popular thinking from 5000 BCE until around the late 1600s explained mental illness as supernatural in nature. Various beliefs over these last thousands of years revolve around the mentally ill person being inhabited by demons, by vapors, or spirits of the dead. Often our ancient forefathers believed that mental illness was the result of one of their gods being angry at the individual, and punishing them with the effects of their sins, manifesting as mental illness.

These ancient surgeons based their treatment methods on the belief that a mentally ill person was possessed and would often use magic, incantations, herbs, prayer, sacrifices, and even threats and bribery to the internal demons in attempts to force it out of the patient. Many people suffering from mental illness were even willing to submit to having their skulls drilled with an auger "to let out" the evil spirits. This technique was called "trepining." The surgeon would then cut into the brain membrane to vent the demons. Patients who did not develop infections and died, most likely behaved the best they could past that point, just to avoid any follow up procedures. Skulls dating back to the year 6500 BCE have been found with holes drilled in them, with many showing signs of healing post-surgery. This practice has continued through time and still has followers in 2016.

It was our Greek friend Hippocrates, in the 4th century BCE, whose wisdom helped to wipe away the spiritual aspect of mental illness and introduce some degree of logic into the discussion. He suggested that mental illness wasn't really caused by spirits or vapors, but rather organic processes in the brain itself.

We can conclude from our own history that mental illness has been with our species from day one. All physicians have wrestled with the causative effects of physical and mental illness. The physicians who contributed to the evolution of our beliefs concerning transsexualism were no different: they had to balance treatment outcomes, versus risks of treatment. I wonder how many physicians, surgeons, midwives, and witch doctors throughout time have been faced with a gravely ill patient who has begged them to "do something" for their pain. Few mortal men and women would have the emotional strength to simply walk away, while most would use all of their skills and talents, (regardless of their usefulness) to help the ailing person.

Some historical accounts make mention of ancient cities filled with beggars and the homeless, and we now know from our own contemporary experience that many of those two groups in our society suffer from mental illness at a higher-than-normal percentage of the population. Whether mental illness is the cause or the effect in this situation is still, six thousand years later, yet to be determined. Solid, well documented accounts of the Roman Caesars show mental illness was common two thousand years ago. Tiberius Caesar's behavior was undoubtedly schizophrenic, and it was apparent that Gaius Caesar Germanicus shared those same traits. The Romans called mental illness "phrenitis," and prescribed opium and wine as treatments to calm the patient. (Not much has changed...lol.)

The practice of bloodletting goes back 2500 years, and is done either through incisions or the use of live leaches. It is still in use today for burn and organ transplant patients. I don't mean to imply that simply because a treatment is old, that it is invalid. On the contrary, I simply ask that these ancient, longstanding treatments adhere to one accepted standard...*to do no harm.*

With the codification of the Nicene Creed by the Council of Nicea in 325 CE, religion began playing a more predominate place in the treatment of mental and physical illness across Europe. For the next thousand years, mental illness was the favorite affliction for those people who were thought to have "sinned" or strayed from the Christian Church. And the inverse was equally true: Only those whom God had personally forgiven returned to their senses. To this day, the religious ritual of exorcism is practiced to free individuals from demonic possession. It is clear from these and numerous other records that physical and mental illness have been a constant throughout human history. We see the very first known community attempt to deal with mental issues in Baghdad, beginning about 795 CE

Unfortunately, there is little other information regarding the patients or cures in those accounts. It would take another five hundred years before the first European facility for mental patients opened. Built in England, that hospital was created by the Priory of the New Order of St. Mary of Bethlehem in the year 1247 CE This very hospital has survived in one form or another, and is still in operation today as the South London and Maudsley National Health Foundation Trust. But over its seven-hundred-and-fifty-year history, it is better known as "Bedlam"

For most of its history it was merely a storage facility for the terminally insane. The English government, much to its credit, has a well-documented history of the affairs of this facility due to the simple fact that public funds have been used for most of its history. St. Bethlehem Hospital is the tail of a society that is too humane and caring to outright kill the mentally ill, and yet too inhumane to take reasonable, decent, and proper care of the patients under their care. Once a person was committed to the hospital, they often suffered more at the hands of the institution than if they had lived on the street. During one inspection of Bedlam, a Scottish patient in the early 1800s was found to have been chained to a wall for twelve consecutive years. Here is a first-hand account of him.

"James Norris, an American marine reported to be 55 years of age who had been detained in Bethlem since 1 February 1800. Housed in the incurable wing of the hospital, Norris had been continuously restrained for about a decade in a harness apparatus which severely restricted his

*movement. The investigator Wakefield stated in his
report:*

*... a stout iron ring was riveted about his neck, from
which a short chain passed to a ring made to slide
upward and downward on an upright massive iron
bar, more than six feet high, inserted into the wall.
Round his body a strong iron bar about two inches
wide was riveted; on each side of the bar was a
circular projection, which being fashioned to and
enclosing each of his arms, pinioned them close to
his sides. This waist bar was secured by two similar
iron bars which, passing over his shoulders, were
riveted to the waist both before and behind. The iron
ring about his neck was connected to the bars on his
shoulders by a double link. From each of these bars
another short chain passed to the ring on the upright
bar ... He had remained thus encaged and chained
more than twelve years.*"

The Bedlam hospital was so unbelievably
horrific a place that the following words are now
eternally associated with the word: MAYHEM,
CHAOS, PANDEMONIUM, CONFUSION,
ANARCHY, DISORDER, DISARRAY,
TURMOIL, COMMONTION, AND UPROAR.

Until very recently, mental illness was only
thought of in relationship to the body. Patients
would go to the same surgeon or midwife in their
village for mental conditions as they would for
physical ailments. Most mental illness, if it could
be kept in check by the person's family, was
never treated. It was the closeness of the patient's

family that kept more functional mentally ill persons out of institutions like Bedlam. But God help that mentally ill person when their parents got old and died, or their circumstances forced them onto the streets. Surgeons and physicians dealt with both body and soul as one entity up until the nineteenth century. It was really only when Sigmund Freud took interest in personality disorders, and stepped away from physical medicine, that treatment for the two states (body and mind) were finally and irrevocably split. Ultimately, some European nations began building and housing the mentally ill in their own versions of Bedlam. And it would take until the late 1700s for a more enlightened viewpoint on mental illness and patients' rights to begin to take hold. The first major victory came in the form of the English Parliamentary Lunacy Act of 1845 and its sister bill, the 1845 County Asylums Act. These acts created a paid commission responsible for the inspection of asylums, and community outreach for the mentally ill. It also established several community facilities for the ill, and worked to remove the mentally ill from poor houses and work houses where many had been improperly imprisoned. It did all this while never defining "lunacy" in any detail.

In the Mental Deficiency Act of 1913 it states: "those deemed idiots, imbeciles or, if under 21, suffering from a lesser degree of mental deficiency, on application of their parents or guardians supported by medical certificates. Other mental defectives might be admitted under a reception order of the judicial authority. As an alternative to being placed in an institution a mental defective might be placed under guardianship."

It is clear from this lack of a proper description of what constitutes mental illness (as we know it today) that there was an unspoken understanding by the public of who qualified as a lunatic and who did not, though it was generally believed that a qualified doctor would certainly be able to tell the difference. It was this base assumption that allowed for the commitment of countless people who were not truly "lunatics," but may have been incarcerated for a host of reasons, none of them related to mental illness. As important as these acts were, it behooves us not to put this into an historical context. Some accounts estimate that humans have been walking the planet for over a million years. While fossil evidence suggests that humans like us have been around for at least eighty thousand years, organized societies have been in existence for the last six-thousand of those years. So, within that specific timeframe, it has only been in the last 175 years that we have begun to take what would be considered "an enlightened view" when it comes to treating people with mental illness. It should come as no surprise that the majority of our knowledge regarding physical and mental illness has only occurred in the last seventy-five years of our entire history on this planet.

Over the course of this last half century, we have advanced our understanding of the human condition by at least a factor of a million-fold. Yet, in spite of everything we have learned, we are still just at the threshold, the very epidermis of discovery about our own human nature. Is it not reasonable then, to suggest that perhaps the best approach to cross-sex identity confusion is to treat these patients conservatively? Would it not then, be the right and just thing for all medical and psychiatric professionals to back off from performing sexual mutilation of this group of patients until we know more about what causes the condition?

Mr. James Norris
1812

CHAPTER FOUR

THE MEDICAL PROFESSION GOES LEGIT

Sigismund Schlomo Freud
Born: May 6, 1856
Freiberg, Austria
Died: September 23, 1939
Graduated University of Vienna 1881

For thousands of years, human knowledge was passed from generation to generation orally. Even after civilizations began to create written language and committed it to some form of medium, the majority of people throughout our history were illiterate. They learned what knowledge there was from the spoken words of their family, friends, tutors, and mentors. As you are aware, the advent of the printing press in the 1500s rapidly escalated the dissemination of knowledge in the world, and with it, medical understanding. Yet it would take another three hundred years for the medical profession to attempt to standardize medical training of practitioners.

Up until the 1850s, the vast majority of people who called themselves "doctors" learned from mentors, who themselves had learned through oral tradition about their profession. As medical schools sprung up around the world, they taught what was known primarily through the oral tradition (lectures) of learning and of what was considered standard knowledge of physicians in that region. This eighty-thousand-year journey of observation, hypothesis, experimentation, theory, research, more observation, and ultimately treatment, truly represents everything that is amazing and great in our species. It was this accumulation of human knowledge that came into focus in the 1800s medical schools. It was Dr. Johann Reil that coined the phrase "psychiatry" in 1808. Psychiatry was first taught in a German medical school starting in the year 1811. In 1844, the American Psychiatric Association was founded.

Unfortunately, the majority of medical schools that sprang up in Europe and the United States during this time were more concerned about the financial health of their schools, rather than the health of their graduates' patients. And the vast number of schools in the world had one entrance requirement: cash. Since few people in the world had what could be called "disposable income," and because no government student loan programs existed, these universities admitted only those who could pay for their degrees. Unlike today, where students must show four to six years of college "pre-med" classes before applying to medical school, many students in those days simply bought their way into medical school with a primary school education. They were able to do this because their families had money. Since money, even amongst the wealthy was not flowing like rivers, and was scarce under almost all circumstances. This reduced the number of classes and time medical students would be able to spend learning. In 1847, Pennsylvania's Medical School, sensing that their students needed more education before practicing on real people, attempted to expand their class time from four to five months. Their student enrollment quickly dropped as a result. The typical medical training in the 1880s and 1890s consisted of two four-month sessions separated by a winter recess. Classes in the majority of schools were typically six or eight hours of lecture per week. To graduate, the student would take a simple exam and get their diploma—if they had paid their tuition! After graduation, it was assumed that the newly educated doctor would find hands-on experience to further their education. They would then go into private practice (if their family had money), or find work in hospitals and public clinics. This style of teaching was really just a more formal structure to the longstanding Oral Tradition, combined with various opportunities of on-the-job training.

Over the next five decades, medical schools teaching criteria eventually expanded and became more standardized in Western societies. It would not be until the end of World War II that the world would see medical and psychiatric training become the rigorous and highly specialized fields we now know. And that was only in the last sixty years.

It was from this world of medical "schools" that the now famous Sigmund Freud, Magnus Hirschfeld, and Harry Benjamin all graduated. While Freud's theories clearly stand out in our human timeline as a milestone for advancements in the study of mental illness, he was only the most well-known of the period. It was his professional belief that much of mental illness was conflict between a human's better natures versus sexual and aggressive tendencies. Though many later psychiatrists in the 1920s and 1930s challenged Freud, proposing contrary theories as the causative factors of mental illness, Freud stands out as the foundation from which the others all sprang. Many of Freud's detractors dispute his theories of mental illness being a manifestation of sexual repression, citing the simple fact that he was practicing among upper-class, sexually repressed society of Vienna in the 1880s. Whether or not this criticism is valid, Freud at least had a theory unrelated to demonic or spiritual possession.

Psychoanalysis, as he defined it, also provided mentally ill patients a safe, non-judgmental place for the very first time in which they could discuss their most intimate thoughts without social repercussion. He also contributed to the field through his structured approach to observation of patients and set what is thought to be the first standard for psychiatry that still exists in one form or another today. He believed that patients could be cured by bringing into the conscious that which was subconscious and in conflict. Psychoanalysis, as Freud defined it, is the foundation used in nearly all other therapeutic treatment methodology today.

And while psychoanalysis is a tremendous advancement over chaining patients to walls, it is only the first step that people with cross-sex identity confusion must take toward releasing themselves of their demons. Anyone who has ever been in traditional psychoanalysis can tell you that talking about one's conflicts does nothing to dispel them. Only after identifying where and what the issues are does the really hard work begin. Freud believed, but never demonstrated empirical evidence, that once the unconscious became conscious, their issues weren't quick to resolve themselves.

And this is the fact that doctors and patients dealing with CSIC must accept. In the later chapters, I will attempt to identify the exact, precise location of where and why CSIC begins.

The doctors that created the diagnosis of transsexual and gender dysphoria found early on that traditional psychiatric therapy had little or no effect on the patient's desire to cross live. Years of couch sitting with the therapist never seemed to help these patients remove the belief that they were souls of one sex trapped in the body of another. Therefore, they concluded, there was nothing that could be done for the patients other than let them live cross sex. None of the doctors then, or now ever questioned the effectiveness of their own therapies to treat this particular mental illness. They did and do believe it is the condition that can't be fixed, not the that their treatment methods that aren't working. But that is precisely what the problem is. Cross Sex Identity Confusion is treatable and curable. It is caused from a failed social structure in childhood. The confusion is hardwired into the person's brain and cannot be fixed by traditional "let's talk about it" Freudian therapy. It can only be fixed by re-wiring how the brain reacts to social situational triggers. Since the majority of all therapeutic and counseling methods are all based, more or less on the Freudian model, they all fail to change personality hardwired schema in the CSIC patient. One way that I have found to be effective is through the use of hypnosis and this is highlighted in a latter chapter.

Traditional therapy just can't fix much more than simple interpersonal issues and conflicts. And when a person comes into a therapist's office with the core of their personality damaged and deranged in early childhood by their parents dysfunctionality and social chaos, the therapist is totally, and completely out of their league with their futile attempts to fix this condition.

But, unlike Freud, I don't just expect us to go on for a year or two talking about the where's and why's of it all. I hope to give you at least one tool to try to repair that damage. I spent fifteen years in one form of psychoanalysis or another. I started out, quite by accident, in therapy with a strict Freudian, and then was happy to move onto a Jungian, a Reichian, a feel-good Marriage Family Counselor, moved back toward more conventional therapy with a quasi-Skinner therapist, and eventually found a graduate of Wardell Pomeroy's Institute for the Advance Study of Human Sexuality. In between these therapists, I looked for answers in religion. I was raised Catholic, converted to Judaism in 1982, left in 1992 and practiced Buddhism for a few years. I then joined a metaphysical church in LA. And through this all I am reminded of the old saying that talk is cheap, and it goes straight to the point of our issue. Every priest, rabbi, therapist, psychologist, psychiatrist and quack has a theory about something. As a long time sufferer of CSIC, all the therapy in the world will only tell me what I already knew… I was confused!

I can see that the wall is not level…please just give me a fucking hammer…that is all I ask!

And that is what this book does, it helps you level your foundation by stripping away all of the false, out of plumb measurements that have built up over the years.

CHAPTER FIVE

THE WRONG TOOL FOR THE JOB

MAGNUS HIRSCHFELD
Born: May 14, 1868
Kolberg, Poland
Died: May 14, 1935
Graduated University of Munich 1891

Between 1864 and 1945, Germany was continuously at war. Their one hundred years of war began in 1864 with the Second Schleswig War, and ending in 1945 with the death of Chancellor Adolf Hitler. Individuals and families are put under tremendous pressure by war, and Germany's constant conflicts deeply affected the

German population. It was out of this violent and tormented period that most of medicine's early pioneers arose.

While Sigmund Freud is seen as the original leader in the modern treatment for mental illness, Magnus Hirschfeld stands out as the first modern-day doctor who tried to do something other than talk about conflicts. After nearly a half century of gay and transsexual activism, Hirschfeld is now hailed as the first medical professional who was openly gay *and* an openly gay advocate. It was this combination that brought him to prominence in the moment that was 1909. His own father was a well-established physician when he first attended the University of Breslan in 1889. He quit the next semester and took a few classes at the University of Stroudsburg in 1890. Then, for reasons known only to him, he quit that school and attended a few classes at the University of Berlin. Moving again after only a few months, Hirschfeld eventually landed at the University of Munich, and with the help of two close friends of his father, was finally awarded a degree in medicine in 1891. Notice that Hirschfeld never completed any one school's curriculum and still became a doctor in less than three years. After graduation, Hirschfeld went into private practice, but made most of his money over the next ten years from writing articles. In 1896, he wrote a then infamous pamphlet *Sappho and Socrates,* an essay on homosexual love. In the following year, he and others founded the Scientific Humanitarian Committee, whose primary goal was to repeal German Penal Code Paragraph 175 as it pertained to homosexuality. It was his intent to change the paragraph to allow for homosexual behavior. He continued working, writing and advocating for homosexual rights over the next few years until 1906, when his name became forever linked with gay activism.

A renowned German General, Kuno Graf von Moltke, sued journalist Maximilian Harden for slander, having been accused in the press by him of being the male lover of Prince Philipp Von Eulenburg. The scandal was a long-running dispute between the general and Harden, who resented the clique called "The Table Circle," which surrounded the Prince. Prince Von Eulenburg had been a target of Harden's journalistic attacks for fifteen years, after former Chancellor Otto von Bismarck gave Harden detailed evidence that members of the Table Circle were mostly homosexuals. The trial that commenced in 1906 was considered the scandal of the century, and every day the European press published sordid details. It was during this trial that Dr. Hirschfeld was asked to testify for the Harden defense. He took the stand and accused General Graf von Moltke of being a homosexual like himself. He based his diagnosis on the Bismarck letters as well as the General's failed relationship with his own wife.

Hirschfeld "outed" Graf von Moltke as being gay. He later recalled that it was a great opportunity for him to show the world that homosexuals could be strong and masculine men like the general. More importantly, by outing Graf von Moltke, Hirschfeld thought it might expedite the repeal of Paragraph 175. What his testimony ultimately did was to ruin Moltke's marriage and force him to retire from the Army. It also ruined

Prince von Eulenburg's relationship with Kaiser Wilhelm. The outing of General Graf Von Moltke, and the resulting resignations of the Kaiser's inner circle would have far-reaching implications for Germany. By 1914, Germany would go into the First World War with its senior-most military and foreign policy strategists all forced into early retirement as a direct result of the Harden trial. It would be the first war German would lose in a hundred years.

In 1910, Hirschfeld began to categorize sexual behaviors in gay men on a scale of 1 – 64. It was in this scale that he coined the condition of "transvestit." The word would eventually become "transsexualism" when translated into English. At the end of World War I, Hirschfeld opened the Institute of Sexual Research in Berlin. The Institute's one goal was to legitimize homosexuality through medical research. It was from his clinic that Hirschfeld and other homosexual doctors worked to better understand the world of sex as it related to homosexuality. It was also the Institute of Sexual Research that attempted to perform the first complete male to female sex change operation.

Prior to 1920, there had been other lesser-known German doctors attempting to treat cross-sex identity confusion through surgery. The first female-to-male surgery was performed in 1912 to remove the person's breasts and ovaries. In 1922, a German doctor, Erwin Gohrbandt, performed what is thought to be the first M-F sex change on a man. As this surgery had never been done before, it was simply a removal of the patient's testicles. The patient, Rudolph Richter, would later change his name to Dora. It would be left to Dr.

Hirschfeld to complete Dora's sexual transformation by performing another surgery in 1933.

Dora

But it was when the Danish painter, Einer Wegener, made the decision to end his life over the emotional pain he suffered from CSIC that the fates of the two men became one. In 1930, doctors from Hirschfeld's clinic began a series of five operations to change Einer from male to female. The last of the five procedures involved inserting female ovaries into Einer's body. Unfortunately for Wegener, his body rejected the tissue and he soon died from an infection.

Einer was a creative man. He obviously grew up with cross-sex identity confusion and suffered from it his entire life. But despite the warm acceptance of his condition from his wife Gerda, Einer continued to be troubled by it, and tried to find ways to cope with his mental illness. When he first sought out professional medical help, he was committed to a sanitarium where the archaic treatments nearly destroyed his mental and physical health. It was not long after that he considered suicide to end his suffering. Dr. Magnus Hirschfeld, in his overzealousness to promote his own beliefs on sexuality, came to Wegener's aid with the offer to perform an experimental surgery. He planned on transplanting a woman's uterus into Wegener, without any previous testing or by first performing experiments on animals. Wegener's surgery is now seen by transsexual advocates in 2016 as a tremendous achievement. What Hirschfeld did was allow Wegener to self-diagnosis his own condition, and then provide the means for self-mutilation. Hirschfeld performed the surgery, without questioning the root cause of Einer's confusion. It is exactly the same thing doctors are doing in 2017.

But I see it as a barbaric medical experiment, done without proper research into the surgery they were about to perform, and without any attempt to cure the causative mental issues behind it. Einer Wegener's surgery was murder committed by a madman.

Wegener died from a massive infection from his surgery, and Magnus Hirschfeld died just four years after Wegener. And while both men are now hailed as pioneers, I see them as victims. Magnus Hirschfeld is a victim of his own ego, as well as his homosexuality. Time and again he was willing to ignore moral decency and social standards to promote his own lifestyle and beliefs. So much so that it cost General von Moltke his distinguished career, his reputation, and his marriage. His maniacal drive to promote homosexuality as being normal may have resulted in the deaths of millions of people in World War One due to the restructuring of German government by the scandal. Hirschfeld's lifelong desire to promote sexual deviance at the expense of everything else ultimately cost Einer his life.

It would not be until 2014 that a successful uterus transplant would take place. Below is a partial list of the various advances in medicine that would have been required for Hirschfeld's 1930 surgery on Wegener to have actually worked. This list does not include the thousands of related surgeries that failed, and other medical research done over these years that led to the few surgeries that *were* successful.

Too often, Hirschfeld is held up by gay and transsexual activists as a hero and pioneer for his bravery and willingness to operate on Einer. But if you read this list, you'll realize that Hirschfeld was operating in complete ignorance of what was necessary for Einer's sex change surgery to be successful.

1930: Alexis Carrel and aviator Charles Lindbergh invent a mechanical heart

1940: Landsteiner and Alexander Weiner revealed the Rh factor based on Landsteiner's previous work,

1940: Linus Pauling confirmed the lock-and-key theory

1945: Robin Coombs, Arthur Mourant and Robert Race developed the 'antiglobulin test'.

1948: Astrid Fagraeus demonstrates that plasma B cells are specifically involved in antibody production

1958: Keith Reemtsma, MD, showed for the first time that immunosuppressive agents would prolong transplant survival in the laboratory setting.

1954: On December 23, the first successful living-related kidney transplant led by Dr. Joseph Murray and Dr. David Hume at Brigham Hospital in Boston:

1959: James Gowans showed that lymphocytes had a role in mediating both cell-mediated and humoral responses.

1960: Edelman, Porter, and Hilschmann elucidated the primary and secondary structure of antibodies.

1962: First successful kidney transplant from a deceased donor, led by Dr. Joseph Murray and Dr. David Hume at Brigham Hospital in Boston.

1963: First successful lung transplant led by Dr. James Hardy at the University of Mississippi Medical Center in Jackson, MS.

1966: First successful pancreas/kidney transplant led by Drs. Richard Lillehei and William Kelly at the University of Minnesota in Minneapolis, MN.

1967: First successful liver transplant led by Dr. Thomas Starzl at the University of Colorado in Denver, CO.

1967: First successful heart transplant led by Dr. Christiaan Barnard at Groote Schuur Hospital in Cape Town, South Africa.

1968: First successful heart transplant in the United States led by Dr. Norman Shumway at Stanford University Hospital, CA.

1972: End Stage Renal Disease Act (ESRD) paves way

for Medicare Coverage of Renal Dialysis and Kidney Transplants.

1975: Kohler and Milstein found the key to monoclonal antibodies.

1981: First Successful heart/lung transplant led by Dr. Brice Reitz at Stanford University

1983: FDA approves Cyclosporine, the most successful anti-rejection medication developed to date

1983: First successful single lung transplant led by Dr. Joel Cooper from the Toronto Lung Transplant Group, at Toronto General Hospital in Canada.

1986: Dr. Michael DeBakey performs the world's first heart transplant in 14 years. (USA)

1986: First successful double-lung transplant led by Dr. Joel Cooper from the Toronto Lung Transplant Group, at Toronto General Hospital in Canada.

1988: FDA approves Viaspan, which greatly extends the preservation of donated livers.

1989: First successful small intestine transplant (a near-total small bowel from a deceased donor) into a child, led by Dr. Olivier Goulet in Paris, France.

1989: First successful living-related liver transplant led by Dr. Christoph Broelsch from Hamburg, Germany, at the University of Chicago Medical Center.

1990: First successful living-related lung transplant led by Dr. Vaughn Starnes at Stanford University Medical Center in Palo Alto, California.

1992: First baboon to human liver transplant performed by Drs. Satoru Todo, Andreas Tzakis and John Fung, at the University of Pittsburgh Medical Center.

1998: First successful hand transplant led by Australian

Dr. Earl Owen and Dr. Jean-Michel Dubernard

2005: First successful partial face transplant led by Dr. Bernard Devauchelle and Dr. Jean-Michel Dubernard in Amiens, France.

2010: The world's first full face transplant took place in Spain.

2014: First successful uterus transplant operation in Sweden.

When Hirschfeld and his sex clinic team cut into Einer, it wasn't a medical treatment, it was a chapter out of Mary Shelly's *Frankenstein*.

Einer Wegener
R.I.P.

"No man chooses evil because it is evil; he only mistakes it for happiness, the good he seeks."

Mary Wollstonecraft Shelley's *Frankenstein: or, The Modern Prometheus* (1818).

CHAPTER SIX

HORMONES IN THE TREATMENT OF TRANSSEXUALS

*1821: A French physician named de Gardanne coins the term "menopause" a century prior to the isolation of the hormone estrogen, and publishes a book "De la ménopause, ou de l'âge critique des femmes". Thus, begins the search for the "cure".

1872: Menopausal women are considered mentally deranged and are classified by Lawson Tait, an influential physician and surgeon of London, as having incurable dementia. In his opinion, relief can be achieved by the use of "an occasional purgative" and "removal from home at frequent intervals" – the asylum!

1890: Merck suggests that menopausal symptoms can be treated with wine, cannabis, opium, and a product made out of powdered ovaries, among others.

1899: An idea was emerging that sex hormones might be involved in menopause. A Parisian woman medicates herself with liquids derived from pigs' ovaries with positive effects.

1929: Estrogen is isolated and identified by Edward Doisy at Washington University in St. Louis.

1930: Water-soluble estrogens are discovered in pregnant mare's urine by a German doctor, Bernhard Zondek. Other researchers reveal that decomposed and hydrolyzed pregnant mare's urine contain estradiol.

1933: The first estrogen replacement product marketed in the US is developed: Emmenin, a product made from the urine of pregnant women. However, it is costly and the search continues for a cheap alternative.

1942: Wyeth's predecessor, Ayerst, receives approval for the patent of Premarin, formulated from the urine of pregnant mares, and is approved by the FDA to market. Initial approval was based on a "replacement" therapy for a woman's depleted estrogen levels.

1943: Wyeth merges with Ayerst, McKenna, and Harrison to produce Premarin®, the world's first conjugated estrogen medicine. * by Jane Allen 2012

No discussion on the medical treatment of transsexuals is complete without a review of the first and primary treatment mode, hormones. Seventy-three years after the process for extracting female hormones from horse urine was developed, the resulting compound, estrogen, is still being used to treat male-to-female transsexuals. Over the last half century, every "wannabe" transsexual has dreamt of getting their hands-on estrogen to begin their process of transition to the opposite sex. Taking estrogen pills has become the de-facto coming of age for those with CSIC. And unlike thirty years ago, when I first tried to have a doctor prescribe the drug, it is now easily and readily available for people who simply self-define as a transsexual. I have read numerous accounts by people that claim they have been prescribed the drug by medical doctors without ever having first been under the care of a psychiatrist. Physicians are now so comfortable with the "limited" side effects of this drug, that they rarely challenge the fledgling transsexual's assertion of their own self-diagnosed condition and need for the medication. I suspect that even a conscientious doctor when, confronted with the CSIC patient who hasn't ever seen a mental health professional, would still prescribe the drug. He would rather monitor the health and safety of the patient, than allow him to buy hormones on the street. Neither scenario is desirable, but one has the potential of serving the patient better than the other.

What doctors have observed over the last three quarters of a century is that males who take female hormones have a softening of their male bodies. Their faces become more rounded, their lips fuller, their facial hair somewhat softer, and their body fat is re-distributed much in the same way as a young woman experiencing puberty. In most men, there is a degree of breast and nipple enlargement. But I've seen the chest/breasts of about a hundred men who were on the drug, and few ever had more than a mouthful of new breast development. What taking hormones most affect are the emotions of the user.

Introducing the hormones of one sex into the other, even if done by choice, is an act of insanity. As much as we've learned about the body over the last hundred years, we don't know enough to be playing around with these critical building blocks of human existence. We do know there are a few dozen types of hormones and they affect a myriad of body functions, with brain chemistry being just one of them. Transsexuals who drop their little yellow or purple pills every day are messing with the single most important organ in their body: the brain. In nearly all cases, these pills are making massive changes in a brain that is already fully developed as male or female. The functioning of the brain is so vast and complicated that in the tiny fraction of what we call human history, we honestly know nothing about it. A brain has 86 billion neurons. Each neuron has between 1,000 to 10,000 synapses, totaling up to 125 trillion synapses in the cerebral cortex alone. Put simply, that 125 trillion is more than 1,000 times the number of stars in our galaxy. Some scientists suggest that just one synapse might contain some 1,000 molecular-scale switches. It is into this amazingly vast mega-structure of neurons and synapses that the "wannabe" transsexual dumps massive doses of the opposite sex's hormones. Gender doctors would have you believe that our personal discomfort and emotional pain overrides all known medical standards of care. Since contemporary scientists still don't completely understand a fraction of *how* the brain works, it would be silly for us not to suggest that the medical establishment hold off on the prescription of cross-sex hormones until we fully understand the basics of brain physiology. But doctors haven't cared in the past, and continue to not care about the long-term effects of hormones on patients.

And let's be real here for one moment. For every patient who demands to be put on female hormones, they are permitting themselves to be used as a lab rat in the experimental treatment of CSIC. For every gender-confused patient that wants the hormones of the opposite sex, there is one more unpaid and willing test subject who has signed a release of liability. It is not only good for the pharmaceutical companies' profit margins, but it also adds to a fuller understanding of side effects in patients that would normally not be done. Hence, this is yet another unofficial, unsanctioned, immoral, and unethical experiment performed by the medical establishment.

The unethical prescribing of cross-sex hormones to mentally ill patients must be brought into question. In 1943, when the cheap production of estrogen began, transsexual patients were still considered to be suffering from a mental illness. Therefore, why would any physician or psychoanalyst prescribe a drug that was not proven to aid in the treatment of that illness? Giving estrogen to males (and testosterone to women) with a mental illness is akin to prescribing LSD to schizophrenics. What has happened to our protectors like the AMA and WHO whose job it is, to keep patients from being prescribed drugs that aren't meant to be used for unrelated conditions. Yet they will let female hormones be used to treat males with a mental condition?

As I document in the next chapter on Dr. Harry Benjamin, he began to give female hormones to male transsexual patients, based on the broad general assumption that it would help them to transition into the desired role of female. He was right in this aspect. Estrogen, and now a host of other steroid-related drugs, are being given to people to help their bodies mask their biological sex, and build a façade of the opposite sex. For much of the last century, since Hirschfeld, there has never been any real attempt at finding a cure for CSIC, but only in finding treatment options to help the patient jump over the abyss that is our human sexual biology and into the role of the opposite sex. Transsexualism is a case study in uncontrolled medical experimentation, not medical treatment.

Another overlooked aspect of hormone treatment for CSIC is the fact that hormones are perhaps the most dangerous and potent drug in the world. Hormones are chemical messengers that produce profound changes in the cells they target. Hormones trigger cell enzymes, which in turn produce widespread consequences within the cells. Cells respond to this hormonal stimulus by causing contraction of muscle tissue and through secretion of cellular by-products. They also have an immediate effect on the ion exchange through the channels that affect the functionality of the cell. Hormones also cause a synthesis of new peptides and proteins within the cell and eventually cause a breakdown of storage molecules. Perhaps the most damaging aspect of taking cross-sex hormones is not just the assault on the patient's body, but on their mind and emotions. Hormones are not candy, but are being prescribed to patients as if they were. CSIC patients are already suffering from emotional pain. They are confused and in crisis about many aspects of their personal lives. Often, their relationships and marriages are on the rocks. Suicidal behavior is very common among persons struggling with gender identity issues. In many cases, CSIC will be the façade of more severe personality disorders and deep psychosis. Patients seeking cross-sex hormones are the very last people on the planet who should be given these mind-altering drugs. Yet it is common practice for doctors to prescribe hormones in the hopes that taking them will lessen the patient's mental disorder. More times than not, hormones are given as a sedative and pacifier, rather than as a cure.

No other mental illness is treated in this same manner. There are a few parallels in medicine, but none of them with such stark contrasts to what the medical profession calls treatment for the transsexual patient.

Dr. Robert Stoller, in his book, *The Transsexual Experiment*, states:

it (transsexualism) raises the intensely felt ethical questions regarding the propriety of using hormones and surgery to change anatomy, "for this is the only condition in which genital, and therefore reproductive *normality* is destroyed for psychological reasons alone."

I can't begin to describe how much I resent his use of the word "normality" as a euphemism for surgical mutilation in the above statement. I've read every one of his books and a sizeable amount of his papers, and he is not a stupid man. But despite the brilliance of his analytical mind, he steps spryly over all ethical questions (that he- himself raises) about destroying patients' anatomies. He then goes on to ignore all ethical issues surrounding these treatments during the time he managed UCLA's sex change clinic. And for CSIC patients to roll into a surgical suite, they must pop the purple pill, estrogen.

There have been valid reasons for the prescription of opposite sex hormones. In some cases, men with prostate cancer have been given female hormones to reduce androgen levels. This was a practical approach, using available tools to help people with medical, rather than psychological, problems. When estrogen entered the market, doctors like Benjamin treated it almost like a new toy, prescribing it for anything and everything. Forget recommended and approved FDA guidelines "Mr. Wilson, take two of these little purple pills twice a day, let me know if there are any side effects, and come back in six weeks so we can see how you're feeling."

If the transsexual patient is lucky, this approach to prescribing estrogen might prove slightly beneficial in that it might offer a sense of resolution to their problems, giving them some emotional comfort. In the middle range of potential risks, there might be a bit of nausea and slight breast tissue development. At the other end of the spectrum, the pills destabilize the patient's fragile emotional state so greatly that they are thrown into a severe depression. But what does it matter? As Stoller makes clear in his book, "As a psychiatric illness, transsexualism is insignificant." And conversely, he implies that transsexual patients are also insignificant.

This aside, it is important for all reading this to understand, that people who are confused by their role in society are not going to eliminate that confusion by attempting to palm themselves off as a member of the opposite sex. Living in the role of a sex involves every aspect of our human existence. It involves, social order, mating, breeding, interpersonal relations, social standing, social class, economics, and even body language. For a confused person to attempt to do this puts them under social pressure that is akin to exposing them to the atmospheric pressure at the bottom of the ocean. Cross sex hormones destabilize a person's mind in unimaginable ways. And they do so at a time, when the person needs every facility to cope with their mind and their world.

November 1864 | July 1913

As Union soldier Albert Cashier, Jennie Hodges marched thousands of miles and fought in many battles in the Civil War

Ireland Calling

www.irelandcalling.ie

CHAPTER SEVEN

DR. HARRY BENJAMIN

Harry Benjamin
Born: January 12, 1885
Berlin, German
Died: August 24, 1986
University of Tubingen 1912

Harry Benjamin became acquainted with Magnus Hirschfeld in 1907, when the latter was doing research for his book on sexuality. Though twenty years Hirschfeld's junior, Benjamin often accompanied him to the gay bars and drag clubs of Berlin. The two men developed what would become a lifelong personal and professional relationship. His time in Berlin with Hirschfeld would have a lasting influence on Harry Benjamin's career. Hirschfeld and Benjamin maintained correspondence long after they both emigrated to the United States. Benjamin eventually ended up in San Francisco, where his practice finally got a foothold. For a number of years, Benjamin was known as a "gerontotherapist", prescribing hormones and chemical cocktails to improve the libidos of aging male patients.

In 1948 Benjamin was approached by Alfred Kinsey about one of his patients. While researching for his book, *Sexual Behavior in the Human Male*, Kinsey met a young boy who did not fit the definitions of homosexual or "transvestite". The boy did not want to just dress as a girl, but wanted to actually live as a girl full time. Though both Kinsey and Benjamin knew of Hirschfeld's operations on Wegener, Kinsey hoped that Benjamin could perhaps work with the boy from a chemical perspective. Benjamin initially worked with two other psychiatrists on the case, but they preferred a more conservative treatment plan different from his. Benjamin quickly disagreed, and after the two other psychiatrists left the case, he convinced the boy's mother to allow him to prescribe the newly available Premarin, a form of female estrogen to the child. The drug, as you remember had only come out on the market seven years previously, and had never been used on a male before. This was long before the American Food and Drug Administration began its forced regulation of drugs and their related usage.

It was from this humble start that Harry Benjamin would become the primary medical physician and advocate to the transsexual community for the next four decades. Over the ensuing years, he found sympathetic therapists, psychiatrists, and surgeons to work with him as he prescribed female hormones and wrote letters approving sex changes for his CSIC patients. At the time, only Denmark legally allowed sex changes to be performed. But slowly, as Benjamin's transsexual-hormone focused practice grew, he began to refer more and more patients for sex change surgery. Denmark was only the beginning; before long, surgeons in Morocco and other countries joined the list of destinations where Benjamin's patients could undergo SRS. Dr. Stanley Biber, a general practitioner and surgeon in Trinidad, Colorado, performed the first SRS surgery in 1969. It would be the first of over four thousand sex reassignment surgeries he would perform.

After years of treating CSIC patients, Benjamin created the Harry Benjamin Sex Orientation Scale. Believing it was necessary to differentiate between transsexualism, and homosexuality, he included his friend Alfred Kinsey's "homosexual scale" as a contrasting reference point. I find the row titled "Psychotherapy" very telling of Dr. Benjamin's viewpoint of the effectiveness of psychotherapy on his patients.

Only in the column for Class II Transvestite does he suggest therapy as "*may be* (my italics) successful if in a favorable environment," However, Benjamin clearly doesn't believe therapy has any merit as a treatment option for any of the other five groups of patients. It is important to keep in mind that Benjamin was simply an old school GP with no training in psychiatry, chemistry or pharmacology.

Doctor Charles Ihlenfeld, a homosexual, and an endocrinologist colleague of Harry Benjamin's for six years, prescribed hormone therapy to well over five hundred of these patients during their association. Dr. Benjamin made note of the fact that in one given year, he prescribed estrogen to over a thousand patients between his offices in San Francisco and New York City.

In Ihlenfeld's book, *Transgender Subjectivities: A Clinician's Guide,* he tries to explain the failure of sex reassignment surgery, and the reason why he would eventually choose to end his affiliation with Benjamin and leave endocrinology altogether.

"Whatever surgery (SRS) did, it did not fulfill a basic yearning (in the patient) for something that is difficult (for the medical profession) to define. This goes along with the idea that we are trying to treat superficially something that is much deeper.... There is too much unhappiness among people who have had the surgery.... Too many end in suicide."

If you have any doubt about the waste of time and money characterizing the current treatment methodology for transsexuals, read this paragraph over a few times. Any transsexual reading this only knows their condition from a singular perspective—their own. Here is a doctor, who worked with Benjamin and hundreds of CSIC patients saying that the medical profession is "trying to treat superficially something that is much deeper"

Once again, remember that when someone takes the time to actually tell you the truth, LISTEN!

By the time Benjamin retired from his transsexual practice, he had treated more patients with estrogen, and referred more patients for SRS surgery than any other physician has to date. He is still considered the father of transsexuality. When he penned his now famous book, *"The Transsexual Phenomenon"* in 1966, it was at the start of the sexual liberation movement and his views on the need to accept and aid the plight of transsexuals found a ready and responsive audience. He did more to bring transsexualism out of the dark alleys of San Francisco and Greenwich Village than any other person has.

And while Dr. John Money floated the idea of a person's "gender" being able to be different from their anatomical sex in a paper in 1955, it was Benjamin who solidified the idea that a person's mental social identity could somehow be different from their birth sex. He referred to this mental personality problem being a "gender problem". He later used the word in the bio for Christine Jorgensen,

"Medically, Christine presents an almost classic case of the transsexual phenomenon or, in other words, a striking example of a disturbed gender role orientation."

Another doctor, Dr. Harry Gershman used the expression "gender identity" in his 1967 paper *"The Evolution of Gender Identity".*

This would be the start of an entire new way of thinking about CSIC in American medical society. Yet neither Benjamin, nor Money or Stoller ever gave scientific evidence that this chasm between personality and anatomic sex actually existed. They all four used the concept of "gender" more to as a means to describe the variances they saw in their patient's expression of self, in relationship to social role stereotypes. But their concept of the word Gender, has now been morphcd by popular culture into a physical reality that is fully separate of anatomical sex. Their creation of Gender being separate from sex, is where the entire medical field took a left turn into the woods we are now lost in. By suggesting that an individual's psyche (as it relates to their sexual identity,) can be factually different from their anatomical sex moves human sexuality into the field of science fiction. Had Benjamin, Money and Stoller been serious medical researchers and not just spectators to the condition, we might very well have gained significant understanding of what the definitive cause of the condition was, rather than what we are left with from their highly simplistic studies. With the idea of Gender now being separate from Sex, (without any empirical research into whether or not it actually is,) has led one therapist after another to take their medical treatment for CSIC patients into the dead-end alley that it is. Throughout history the roles of men and women in society have fluctuated, and both sexes have taken on or discarded certain stereotypical sex roles with that flux. But neither that nor CSIC patient's obsession of opposite sex roles cannot be taken to mean that the mental sex is different from the physical sex. Human biology can't be broken apart and separated. I offer no other evidence of this than the fact that our species has lasted nearly 2 million years because of our fixed, two-sex biology. If Gender identification could actually be able to be broken apart from anatomy, then that flaw in our biological DNA make up would certainly be a conditional risk for the demise of our entire species. Our identity is our sex, and that is why we have lasted as a solitary species for this long. Any confusion or discomfort a person has around social role verses anatomy is certainly mental in origin. While there have been two poorly funded medical attempts to identify if there are brain differences between CDIC patients and normal patients, these have found nothing of significance.

Looking at Dr. Benjamin's life in retrospect, it is clear that his twenty-five-year friendship with Magnus Hirschfeld, his early work prescribing hormones and vitamin supplements to treat his patient's libidos, his relationship to sex researcher Alfred Kinsey, and the majority of his patients having some form of cross-sex identity confusion helped to shape his professional beliefs and fashioned the treatment options he offered. By numerous patients' accounts, he was a warm and non- judgmental man who legitimately cared about their wellbeing. I, sitting here in 2016, cannot find fault with anything the doctor did. Honestly, I can't.

But let me ask you one question. When we see old monster movies, and all the villagers storm the castle to kill the monster, why are they all carrying pitchforks, sickles, and axes?

On the surface, it seems like a silly question that has nothing to do with our topic or with Dr. Benjamin. But I assure you, it has everything to do with him, and how people confused about their sexuality and "gender" are now treated by the medical profession.

Let me explain: When we watch those movies, with the villagers looking to do away with the monster, they are armed with tools you would find at a hardware store, or more specifically, sitting around their farms. That's because, when they finally get around to killing the monster, they use the only tools they have.

Dr. Harry Benjamin began treating CSIC patients with the only tools he had. For his acceptance tool, he cruised the gay bars and drag clubs of Berlin with Magnus Hirschfeld, where they clearly developed friendships with other gay men. For his treatment tool, he utilized hormones from his treatments of aging patients for libido problems. For the patients who could not be satisfied with just taking hormones, he chose the sex change procedure tool, also from his friend Hirschfeld's medical experimentation on Einer Wegener.

His professional disdain for the effectiveness of psychotherapy on CSIC clearly dates back to the period in which he received his medical diploma. Benjamin really represents the last graduates of the fly-by-night era of medical schools. In 1912, when Benjamin graduated from the University of Tubengen, Dr. Freud and his new science of psychoanalysis were still relatively unknown to the medical profession. Those physicians who were aware of the emerging field may not have seen any real value in it. Even when Benjamin wrote his 1966 book on transsexuality, Dr. Benjamin placed *zero* value on that psychoanalysis, even after six decades of development. In his Standards of Care for transsexuals, he states:

"Psychotherapy is not an absolute requirement for triadic therapy."

What is more remarkable is that he advises medical professionals dealing with CSIC patients *not to cure* them of their confusion and ideation, but to offer options to live as a transsexual. It is clear that in Dr. Benjamin's mind, only hormones and surgery could fix gender dysphoria, ignoring the resolution of childhood mental/social conflicts. It is also telling that when you read his Standards of Care (available online), sections four, five, and six, which appear in the first two pages, are dedicated to criteria for hormones treatment. It is precisely because of the focus of his practice at the time he was referred a boy by Kinsey, that he took the direction he did. It was the combination of his old-school medical education and lack of psychoanalytical training that points to the simple fact that Dr. Harry Benjamin used the limited tools he had at hand to slay the monster that is transsexualism. He never looked for the real answer to the CSIC riddle, and as a result treated thousands of confused patients with pills and surgery. By taking CSIC patients and turning them into quasi semi-women he created his own army of monsters, shunned by their own families and made outcast by the rest of society. Had he been the compassionate man they said he was, thousands would have not traveled down this road.

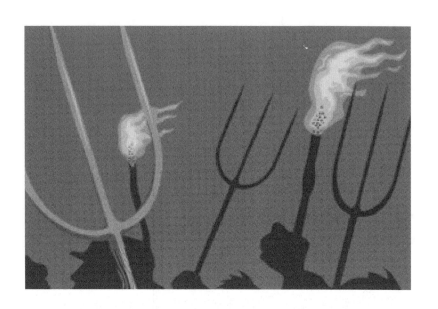

CHAPTER EIGHT

DR. JOHN MONEY

John William Money
Born: July 8, 1921
Morrinsville, New Zealand.
Died: July 7, 2006
Victoria University of Wellington 1944
Harvard University 1952

The city of Morrinsville sits in central New Zealand and was home to the Maori tribes before Western European settlers invaded the island. Its climate was ideal for cattle ranching and soon became a dairy region for the island. After the Great War ended in 1917, many of New Zealand's sons were granted land tracks in the region to help them with their mental rehabilitation. It was in this bucolic environment that John Money attended university during the World War Two. Dr. Money's love of his native country never left him, and he would ultimately leave a sizeable collection of aboriginal and contemporary art to the New Zcaland University before he died. He was considered by his colleagues to be a man of morals, intellect and discipline. And this discipline shows itself in his meticulous studies on how sex, anatomy and roles interplay.

I have just finished re-reading five of his primary books, and I am struck by how clear, concise and articulate Dr. Money was. He is truly the first Margaret Mead of contemporary sex. Yet his writings suggest a man completely obsessed with cracking the code behind social roles, social interaction and human gender. Sixty-four years after John Money graduated from Harvard with his Ph.D. there still exists much controversy surrounding his methods and personal ethics. Whatever else that can be said about this man, he was the first western-trained psychologist to study gender confusion as a specialty.

That in the entire history of our species that he was *the first in his field to view sex from a twentieth century perspective.*

Perhaps it was his total obsession with all things sex and gender that ultimately led to his personal downfall.

It was John William Money who first articulated what Freud, Kinsey, Hirschfeld, and Benjamin hadn't even begun asking. Although Hirschfeld and Benjamin routinely treated CSIC patients, it was Money who looked beyond the symptoms and in trying to figure out what was triggering their behavior, introduced the concept of *gender* into the treatment of transsexuals.

"All those things that a person says or does to disclose himself or herself as having the status of boy or man, girl or woman, respectively. It (gender) includes, but is not restricted to sexuality in the sense of eroticism. Gender role is appraised in relation to the following: general mannerisms, deportment and demeanor; play preferences and recreational interests; spontaneous topics of talk in unprompted conversation and casual comment; content of dreams, daydreams and fantasies; replies to oblique inquiries and projective tests; evidence of erotic practices, and, finally, the person's own replies to direct inquiry."

In 1955 Money wrote an article hypothesizing gender identity as "malleable" in the individual, and he continued to develop his research and practice around this solitary principle for the rest of his fifty-year career. Why he and Benjamin used the term gender to describe personal identity and social roles was never fully explained.

"There's no by-passing the gender identity fork. It is practically impossible for a person to develop any sense of identity at all without identifying as either a male or female, and the gender identity gate locks firmly behind them. Yet, in a way, the fork must be straddled. You had to construct both male and female internal models-

schemas in your brain, concepts of what it means to be a male, and what it takes to be a female."

This "gender identity gate," he speculated, occurs around the age of 18 months, and because it happens at such an early age, he believed that it is a threshold that could never be transversed again after crossing.

So, let's stop here for a moment and change perspectives. Instead of looking at this precept from a psychological angle, let's look at this from the perspective of a patient whom Dr. Money has diagnosed as a true transsexual. The mere fact of the diagnosis immediately eliminates all other treatment options. In Dr. Money's therapeutic belief, the patient's "gate" has now closed and can never reopen. Why they would he suggest that the patient forego living in the opposite sex role and return to living in the role of his or her birth sex if he believed the gate was closed? With this diagnosis fixed in the doctor's mind, his CSIC patients will live their lives as proof of Money's belief. The rigidity of his closed gender gate theory becomes a self-fulfilling destiny.

Demented person that I am, I am seeing a black and white movie in my mind of passengers boarding an old steam train, and the conductor (played by Dr. John Money) yelling out, "The gender gate has closed; all passengers will disembark in Baltimore for a sex change before continuing. The gender gate has closed! Next and final stop for this train…Baltimore."

Prior to Dr. Money's theory, gender was not a personal attribute, but first appeared in language, based around biology dating back thousands of years. While there are no hard and fast rules in those languages around what constitutes a word's gender, or how to determine the gender of a new word that enters the vocabulary, the thirty-eight languages that still use word-gender generally base the sex of the person most associated with that word. The medical profession never really associated gender with individual behavior before Benjamin and Money.

Mary Twain wrote:

"In German, a young lady has no sex, while a turnip has. Think what overwrought reverence that shows for the turnip, and what callous disrespect for the girl. See how it looks in print—I translate this from a conversation in one of the best of the German Sunday school books:

Gretchen. "Wilhelm, where is the turnip?
Wilhelm. "_She_ has gone to the kitchen."

Gretchen. "Where is the accomplished and beautiful English maiden?"

Wilhelm. "*It* has gone to the opera."

Gender stems from Aristotle's Greek term, *genos*. In Latin *genitive generis* translates as "race, kind, family, stock, rank, order, species, and sex." The sex and gender of a person were always one and the same, since the words were used interchangeably until the middle of the last century. It is the separation of the meaning of gender from the anatomic sex of a person that completely changes the treatment options for CSIC patients. Prior to Dr. Money's theories, the meaning of "gender" was a social attribute for *the group* of that particular sex, not an individual attribute. It was certainly not meant as a personality trait that was malleable and fluid. We should not be surprised that Dr. Money developed the theory of gender being an individual trait. With a clientele of anatomically male "transsexuals" presenting in varying degrees of women's dress, it likely further slanted his perspective. Under these circumstances, it's easy to see how any doctor would begin to believe that male/female role identity, as it relates to one's sex, can be fluid and different from their anatomy.

Keep in mind that psychology was (and still is) creeping out of thousands of years of superstition and ignorance. To give you some historical perspective on just how backwards medicine was during this period, while Benjamin was developing his gate theory, another doctor named Walter Freeman was traveling across the

United States in his personal van, infamously named the "lobotomobile". For $25 dollars, he would perform transorbital lobotomies on mentally ill patients, the majority of which had the procedure done without any anesthetic.

Dr. Freeman & his Lobotomobile

By the time, Freeman retired in 1967, he had performed lobotomies on four thousand patients, by some undocumented accounts he performed over 5,000. Unfortunately, nearly twenty percent of his patients had major physical and mental damage caused by his treatment, and over 15% (514) of his patients died on the table from his procedure. I bring up Freeman because the medical profession let this bona-fide serial killer run lose around the country from 1936 until 1967.

So, for those in the LGBT community that feel comfort in the fact that the APA, and AMA now support self-diagnosis and sex changes of transgender people, remember the name Walter Freeman. And the fact that these very same medical associations, looked away while Freeman roamed the country for thirty years, killing people.

Benjamin published *The Transsexual Phenomenon* the year after Freeman retired. The American medical profession has rarely called out one of their own, and Drs. Freeman and Money were no exception. People with "mental illness" were thought to be dysfunctional, not aberrant. Cross dressers, homosexuals, and CSIC people were, in 1955, still viewed as moral deviants rather than suffering from personality disorders. When a patient presented themselves to Dr. Money as a normal person who could hold down a job, but wanted a normal life as the opposite sex, they weren't placed in the same category as a patient who thought themselves to be Napoleon, i.e., mentally ill.

CSIC is a personality disorder and thus qualifies as mental illness. That was until the highly politically motivated board that makes us the Diagnostic and Statistic Manual of Mental Disorders (DAM) decided to remove it from their list of mental illness. What I believe tripped up Dr. Money and others who have focused their medical practice around this field, is the fact that this class of patients isn't your typical bunch of crazies. In 1955, homosexuals in drag were quickly eliminated from this category of patients. Those remaining were patients who, because of rigid societal standards, simply wanted to live as the opposite sex.

The few living full time as the opposite sex would have had to be highly functional individuals, who could live, pass and function in the structured society that 1950s American was. Therefore, if they weren't running around the streets being a threat to themselves and others, they weren't considered mentally ill. Years later, this medical perspective was still accepted and expanded upon when it was further elaborated on the term transsexual as:

". . . a sense of persistent identification with, and expression of, gendercoded behaviors not typically associated with one's sex at birth, and which were reducible neither to erotic gratification, nor psychopathological paraphilia, nor physiological disorder or malady. The self-applied term was meant to convey the sense that one could live not pathologically in a social gender not typically associated with one's biological sex, as well as the sense that a single individual should be free to combine elements of different gender styles and presentations, or different sex/gender combinations. At one level, the emergence of the 'transgender' category represented a hair-splitting new addition to the panoply of available minority identity labels; at another level, however, it represented a resistance to medicalization, to pathologization, and to the many mechanisms whereby the administrative state and its associated medicolegal-psychiatric institutions sought to contain and delimit the socially disruptive potentials of sex/gender non-normativity. Having an intelligible social identity is the means by which an individual body enters into a productive relationship with social power. Thus 'identity politics,' the struggle to articulate new categories of socially viable personhood, remains central to the consideration of individual rights in the United States, and to the pursuit of a more just social order. The emergence of 'transgender' falls squarely into the identity politics tradition." * (2010 Jack Dresser MD)

While investigating CSIC, Money associated the concept of" nature vs. nurture" into the gender mix. He eventually declared that CSIC was the total result of nurture, rather than what many today believe. It was this declaration that has ultimately tarnished Dr. Money's career, and his writings on the subject of transsexualism.

Dr. Money was approached by a couple named Reiner in 1967 to help them with a problem. During the procedure to circumcise their young infant twin sons, the penis of one was accidently burnt off. Dr. Money quickly suggested that the boy who lost his penis be raised as a girl. The case would give Money the fertile ground to prove his theory, and he jumped at the opportunity to work on the case. After the parents agreed Dr. Money's recommendation, he graciously agreed to manage the case and started to administer female hormones to the boy. This case has been widely reported, and therefore, I don't feel it necessary to delve into specifics in this short space.

Had everything worked out as Dr. Money knew in theory they should have, he would have been heralded as a pioneer in the field. But life and gender are infinitely more complex than he anticipated, and everything that could go wrong with his treatment of the Reiner twins did. The treated twin boy/girl never took to "her" new identity and eventually chose to live as a male, while the other twin never fully accepted his sister as a boy. Worse yet, the two boys would later publicly denounce Dr. John Money, claiming he had emotionally, sexually and physically abused them during his private psychotherapeutic sessions when they were young. Ultimately, both men would kill themselves before reaching the age of forty. Damn, it just doesn't get any worse than this, does it? And when I first read about these two boy's lives and Money's experiment, I thought to myself "What an asshole Money was!"

But for the sake of argument, I would like to step back a moment from the charges of child abuse and look at why his experiment/treatment might not have worked. For people who want to believe that gender dysphoria is caused by nature, something is damaged or defective in our bodies. They look to this case as prime example that the theory of nurture causing gender issues is wrong, and conveniently don't look past the later charges leveled against Money. However, I believe we must look deeper at the Reiner family structure for answers. The fact that the gender assigned boy/girl never adapted to the role of "Brenda" helps prove in some doctors' and transsexual advocates' minds that gender dysphoria is biological and therefore can't be cured or fixed by therapy. Yet, both Dr. Money, and later Dr. Robert Stoller, continued to suggest the prime cause of gender issues is directly related to the family structure and dynamics, despite the outcome of the Reiner case. I am assuming that when all this shit hit the fan, Dr. Money was so busy trying to defend himself from his critics that he didn't have the mental clarity to try to figure out why the Reiner girl never accepted her new role. If he had, I believe he would have realized that the Reiner family structure was too functional and too normal to produce a failed cross-sex identity. I personally suspect that the twin's father, Mr. Reiner, was too normal and strong of a male role model, and Mrs. Reiner too normal and strong of a female role model to produce the desired effects on the affected twin's mental makeup. The boy never adapted to the role because the gender gate was closed, and it closed with both boys firmly entrenched in male identities. Though we will never know, I think there is a chance that either or both of the parents never fully accepted the change, and in very subtitle ways, kept relating to "her" as him. Several studies since this case have attempted to identify many common situational conditions that all transsexual's families have in common. To date, these limited case studies have not been able to identify any. Another thing this case proves is how painful and just awful CSIC is on the individual. Brenda Reiner was in all actuality a transsexual, a transsexual created by the doctor who accidentally burnt off his penis. Dr. Money who took that accident as an opportunity to test his theories is what actually made Brenda a transsexual. Brenda Reiner's life was filled with the torment of being an (sic) anatomical female but feeling like a man inside. She/he felt like a man inside for exactly the reasons that Money *was* attempting to prove. Money succeeded in proving his theory that CSIC was the result of family nurture dynamics, but for all the wrong reasons. He died never understanding that his theories *were* valid. Given how he is now known to have intervened not only the Reiner family but in other families as well, the evidence is pointing to the fact that Money had, and would abuse anyone in an effort to prove his theories. One must ask if he is any different from Hirschfeld performing a sex change on Einer

Wegener in 1933, or Dr. Benjamin passing out female hormones to thousands of men before having conducted any medical research first to identify risks. Is John Money's contributions to the medical and psychological treatment options of transsexuals no less naive, or horrific, or slanted than theirs?

Given the ultimate outcome of his medical intervention in the Reiner case, it is ironic that the title of one of his books is *Unspeakable Monsters: In All Our Lives.*

Mrs. Reiner and twin sons

CHAPTER NINE

Dr. ROBERT J. STOLLER

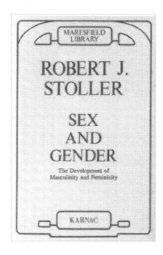

Robert Jesse Stoller
Born: December 15, 1924
Bronxville, New York
Died: September 6, 1991
University of California San Francisco 1948

Anyone familiar with Los Angeles knows the name of one of its most iconic streets: Sunset Boulevard. The street starts innocently enough on the east side of LA near the Chinatown and the 110 Freeway. It then leisurely winds its way in a North-Easterly direction through the recently gentrified neighborhoods of Echo Park and Silver Lake. About the time you see the historic Vista Theater on the right hand side of the street, Sunset gets a quick kiss by Hollywood Boulevard where it ends, and takes off running towards the west. The pace of the street quickly ramps up as it speeds its way through the tourist-infested Hollywood section of the route. Here, you see all of the gay gyms, drunks, druggies, and whores welcoming you to LA. The street becomes *the* "Sunset Boulevard" about the time you see the ever-popular Griddle Café on the south side of the street near the bustling intersection of Fairfax. And you know you are alive and living the life when you catch a quick glimpse of the iconic Directors Guild building on the left, then the Laugh Factory and the immensely popular Greenblatts Deli on the right. And about the time that you think you can't be more chic, you pass the Skybar's gigantic doors on the left, followed by three blocks of notoriously notorious eateries where only the rich and famous take Sunday brunch to talk about their latest film projects. When Sunset takes a quick left, and then right where Holloway Avenue intersects, all true Los Angelinos look to the south side of the street, where River Phoenix died of a drug overdose on the sidewalk in front of The Viper Room. At North Doheny Avenue, Sunset shakes off the big city attitude and assumes a more elegant persona as it slaloms through the manicured lawns of Beverly Hills. Rushing past the multi-million dollar homes of the gated Brentwood neighborhood, drivers are mercilessly bounced from one pothole to another while flying past the UCLA campus, and then under the always congested 405 freeway. Now overwhelmed with pride in its pedigree, Sunset saunters boastfully through the "you can't afford to live here if you have to ask" neighborhoods of Brentwood Park and Riviera. And if all this wasn't enough, Sunset Boulevard still insists on boasting about its last (and in some minds finest) community, Pacific Palisades. It is here, on the west side of Los Angeles, that this amazing forty-mile street finally concludes at Pacific Coast Highway. And what every driver who has ever driven this street will tell you is just how windy and treacherous some sections of it are. There are hundreds of blind curves and driveways obscured by hedges, scrubs, and fencing. Despite the heavy presence of motorcycle police through the Boulevard, drivers often use the street as an urban Formula One racetrack. Most days there are numerous accidents along this route.

It was under this circumstance that Dr. Robert Jesse Stoller died on September 6, 1991. He pulled his car out of his own Sunset Boulevard driveway and was killed by an oncoming vehicle. A common accident on this remarkable street. The accident ended the career of a uniquely American doctor who had spent fifty years researching human sex and gender. Though not among the early pioneers to study gender, Stoller does represent a paradigm change in not only the length of his medical training, but also the depth of his medical and psychiatric understanding. When Robert Stoller left the military at the end of World War II, fate guided him to the open arms of University of California Los Angeles, where in 1954, he would go on to write nine books and over 100 research papers. It was in this fertile ground of contemporary Los Angeles that he would question the most basic medical and mythical concepts about sex, sexuality and human gender.

Masters and Johnson (M&J) began interviewing people about their sex lives in 1957, and their work paralleled Stoller's deep dive into sex and gender. M&J published their groundbreaking book, *Human Sexual Response,* in 1966, the same year Dr. Benjamin published *The Transsexual Phenomenon.* Much in Stoller's writings follows the same path as Money's , but nothing in Stoller's research ever discredited him to the degree that Money's work on the Reiner family did. And despite the fact that Money and Stoller were close in age, the latter's writing and research seems more modern than Money's. This difference could result from the differences in environments and education. Harvard on the conservative East Coast greatly influenced Money, while Stoller attended University of California Los Angeles, on the more liberal West Coast. In addition, Money's patients had more conservative backgrounds, while Stoller's emanated from a gay-friendly, artistic environment, dominated by the film industry.

Unlike the doctors profiled earlier here, Stoller was an American, and formally trained in modern psychiatry. He based his original work on the teachings of his idol, Sigmund Freud. But he didn't just use one style of treatment. He would eventually introduce Jung, Skinner, Kinsey and others' ideas into his treatment. As he continued to study transsexuals and gender confusion, he employed a solid analytical approach. So it was in sunny Southern California that he published his book, *Sex and Gender* in 1968. The book was from his years of analysis and research of patients in the Los Angeles area. More interesting is the fact that this book was not only well received in the medical community, but also by the general population. It was this initial core research data, and the absence of any other detailed research on the subject (that met his formal research standards) that inspired Stoller to look deeper into the subject of transsexuals. Out of that second look came his next significant book, *Sex and Gender, Volume II: The Transsexual Experiment* in 1974. The book includes what I see as a telling preface:

> **"Can transsexualism tell us anything about normal development? For some people, this is an interesting but bizarre condition, a shoddy amusement; one that is easily lost in frivolous details. To do so, however, is to miss the opportunity for an 'experiment' we would never ourselves dare perform, which may help us study the unfolding of masculinity and femininity in less aberrant people."**

He writes this after nearly fourteen years research on gay and transsexual patients. Yet in his mind there was still "normal" and "aberrant" behavior. Despite his professional opinion, he became a staunch advocate for removing homosexuality from psychology texts as a mental illness and a form of deviant behavior. While Money helped to separate gender from sex, it was Stoller (1964) whose work introduced "Core Gender Identity" into psychoanalytic literature and the minds of Western psychiatrists. Ten years after writing *The Transsexual Experiment*, Stoller expanded on the causative factors stating that they might occur as a result of family dynamics during the childhood phases of individuation and separation. This came from the theories of Margaret Mahler (Mahler, Pine, & Bergman, 1975).

In the introduction to his second volume, Stoller writes:

"I see male transsexualism as an identity per se.... To me, transsexualism is the expression of the individual's true self."

However, Stoller immediately tries to distance his belief from other common forms of cross-sexual identity confusion.

"On the other hand, the perversions of gender identity, such as fetishistic cross dressing, are compromises cemented over an earlier self that will never again be seen because the defense is so keenly pleasurable."

It took Money to break gender out of anatomical sex, and now Stoller reconstitutes that idea into a completely separate personality structure. Core Gender Identity quickly became accepted by the medical community as part of human nature. Prior to this point in time, if you asked a doctor to list the biological traits of human sexuality, most would answer:

- Chromosomal
- Hormonal
- Anatomical

But Hirschfeld, Kinsey, Money and Stoller added two more, non-biological categories to the first:

- Gender
- Sexual preference

These two do not relate to the previous three, but with Stoller's influence, the latter became permanently glued to the former. It would be this inclusion of the latter two elements into the core belief of the bases of human sexuality that has since influenced the vast majority of medical and psychological doctors, progressive medical associations, teachers and sexologists. Stoller also theorized that gender identity can be separate from sexual orientation. This was very convenient, since many of the people that presented themselves to Stoller as male-to-female transsexuals claimed not to be sexually attracted to males. This one issue is a major "red flag" that Stoller and all the others totally missed. I discuss this further in a later chapter.

Based on John Money's closed gate theories, he, Howard Jones and Milton Edgerton started America's first gender identity clinic in 1965. The following year, John Hopkins University announced that the trio had succeeded in performing their first male-to-female sex change. Not long after, Robert Stoller began the University of California at Los Angeles sex and gender clinic, followed by another such clinic at Stanford University. Lastly, Dr. Stanley Biber of Trinidad, Colorado, began offering sex changes in his private clinic in 1969. Biber performed over 3500 SRS surgeries by the time he retired thirty-five years later.

After starting the UCLA clinic, Stoller used many of its new patients for his continued research into sex and gender, which informed his second book. Despite the establishment of six clinics in the United States offering sex changes, there was still staunch resistance from some sectors of the medical profession. Remember that John Money's work on gender helped initiate the sex change program at Johns Hopkins. What is surprising that one of America's leading physicians, Dr. Paul McHugh began to question the long-term prognosis of their post-surgical transsexual patients, and ordered an analysis of Hopkin's own post-surgical patients, causing things to unravel for medical proponents of sex change surgery.

Dr. McHugh is an extraordinary doctor and compassionate man. In 1975, he was appointed Henry Phipps Professor of Psychiatry and Director of the Department of Psychiatry and Behavioral Sciences at Johns Hopkins University School of Medicine. He also served as Psychiatrist-in-Chief of the Johns Hopkins Hospital. It was from his position at the hospital that he requested the follow-up analysis of the outcomes of their SRS patients. Finally in 1977, that analysis, completed by Drs. John Meyer and D. J. Reter concluded that, *"sex reassignment surgery confers no objective advantage in terms of social rehabilitation."*

More importantly, their report showed that 47% of all post-surgery patients had attempted suicide, with approximately 10% of their 50 patients ending their lives. This is a ridiculously high number statistically, and can't be overlooked as insignificant. Suicide among transsexuals was nearly 100 times higher than that among any other group. This analysis was from 1977, and these numbers are still valid based on recent studies.

Dr. McHugh used this analysis as rationale to eventually close the Hopkins sex change clinic in 1979. While the rest of the medical establishment has intentionally turned a blind eye and ignored the outcomes of SRS, Dr. McHugh has become one of the most vocal medical opponents of the these insane procedures. As a direct result, he has become a favorite target for the extreme left "social justice warriors". Their scathing attacks try to discredit him not only professionally, but also personally. They do this, all the while praising Hirschfeld's murderous experimentation on Einer Wegener.

I have read the report by Dr's. Meyer and Reter and it showed no particular bias in their wording. They did what all good scientists do—they looked at the data and presented conclusions based on numbers.

McHugh once said of SRS that it is *"the most radical therapy ever encouraged by twentieth century psychiatrist...similar to the once widespread practice of frontal lobotomies."*

With the tide of gay and transsexual acceptance having reached the White House, McHugh has been demonized by transsexual activists for having an opinion that is contrary to their political correctness.

Eventually, all of the other university clinics closed their sex change clinics. And in spite of the growing data that demonstrate post-surgical adjustment as very low, more private clinics have opened in the United States, Thailand, Casablanca, and Europe. Even Iran, a conservative Muslim country, began to offer sex changes (after a religious edict stated that there was nothing in their holy book that prohibited it.) While Dr. Stoller added tremendously to the depth of statistical understanding of CSIC, he failed to get to the root causes of the condition.

Perhaps when a man enters a doctor's office dressed as a woman, wanting to/willing to give up his penis *and* his male privilege, it is all just too jarring for people. Perhaps the picture CSIC patients present is just too aberrant. Even experienced people like Benjamin, Money and Stoller seem to have focused on the superficial and controversial aspects of this condition, and somewhere along the way, lost interest in what causes it. I can't help but wonder what went through Stoller's mind on the day he closed his sex change clinic. How bittersweet it must have been to have spent years studying the condition, then operating on those he studied, only to realize that you didn't really understand the condition, or the people, or the cause of it...at all.

CHAPTER TEN

Dr. Joesph Mengele

Don't it make your brown eyes blue.

Joesph Mengele
Born: March 16, 1911
Gunzburg, Germany
Died: February 7, 1979
University of Munich 1937, PhD
University of Frankfurt 1938, M.D.

As I sit to write this chapter on medical experimentation, I'm laughing aloud and wondering… what is it about German doctors and medical experiments?

In the overall scheme of things, Dr. Joseph Mengele was and is a nothing. He is a foot-note at the bottom of the page, deep inside a book on one war's atrocities. He neither had an outstanding military career, nor a brilliant medical career. Unlike notable German officers like Field Marshal Erwin Rommel, Mengele used and abused his role in the army as a personal playground in a vain attempt to further his personal understanding of genetics and eugenics. While lesser ranking German officers were ultimately held accountable for their sadistic behavior, Dr. Mengele managed to escape Germany after the war, and lived to old age under various names and identities in South America. During his time as a doctor in various Nazi concentration camps, he focused some of his experiments on twins and disease. He sought out thousands of young twins from the various concentration camps and had them sent to him for experiments. During the two and a half years he worked in the camps, records show that he was responsible for killing over three thousand twins. Another favorite experiment of Dr. Mengele was attempting to produce the perfect blue eye color for the Aryan race. He would inject various chemical compounds directly into the eyes of living prisoners, and then after killing the subject, dissect their eyes.

The world would be a better place too if Dr. Mengele were the only sadistic Germans had unleashed during the war, but he wasn't. Germany's most infamous sadistic doctor was Karl Brandt.

Brandt was an intimate confidant of Adolf Hitler who, along with Himmler, was responsible for planning the mass executions for which the Nazis are notorious.

It was Dr. Brandt who set the example for all the other little sadistic Nazi doctors. If only the Third Reich were alone in such unspeakable research, but nearly every other country is guilty of a host of chemical, organic and biological experiments on prisoners and general populations. Japan's Unit 731 killed so many prisoners and civilians in their experiments that they actually lost track of the number, now estimated at over 300,000.

Dr. Karl Brandt

Medical experimentation on involuntary subjects was so rampant during the World War II that when that it finally ended, the medical profession—after examining its own lack of professional standards—drafted the Nuremburg Code of ethics.

It is comprised of these ten points:

1. Required is the voluntary, well-informed, understanding consent of the human subject in a full legal capacity.

2. The experiment should aim at positive results for society that cannot be procured in some other way.

3. It should be based on previous knowledge (such as an expectation derived from animal experiments) that justifies the experiment.

4. The experiment should be set up in a way that avoids unnecessary physical and mental suffering and injuries.

5. It should not be conducted when there is any reason to believe that a risk of death or disabling injury is implied.

6. The risks of the experiment should be in proportion to the expected humanitarian benefits.

7. Preparations and facilities must be provided that adequately protect the subjects against the experiment's risks.

8. The staff who conduct or take part in the experiment must be fully trained and scientifically qualified.

9. The human subjects must be free to immediately quit the experiment at any point when they feel physically or mentally unable to continue.

10. Likewise, the medical staff must stop the experiment at any point when it is apparent that continuation would be dangerous.

And while there were other national medical standards in place before that time, many were updated as in direct response to medical atrocities committed during the war. The above standards address medical experimentation, rather than medical research. In retrospect, I don't think they went far enough , but given the circumstance, I am not surprised. Had involuntary medical experimentation ended with the publishing of the Nuremburg Code, we would all be breathing easier right now. But it didn't, and since WWII ended, there have been hundreds of known cases where unsuspecting people have been subjected to dangerous, deadly, mind-altering, deforming, crippling and lethal tests by doctors around the globe. Some, like Walter Freeman were done in full sight of the medical establishment, while others were backed by covert government agencies like the American Central Intelligence Agency. I had originally intended to include an appendix of these medical experiments, but the shortest list I could find comprised over 32 pages. On this "short" list were descriptions of some of the most blood-curdling experiments I've ever read. I decided against including them as they would have taken too much emphasis off my main point.

Needless to say, Dr. Joseph Mengele was not the first nor the last sadistic doctor to run amuck since 1939.

I am certain that you can see where I am going with all this.

When we take a close look at the primary treatment for transsexuals, we are looking at SRS. And as we now approach the hundred-year anniversary of Magnus Hirschfeld's attempted surgery on Einer Wegener, I don't believe it is unreasonable for us to stop, take a breath and ask ourselves, "Is SRS reasonable and ethical for what we know about this mental condition in 2016?" And before we can answer that question, we must first ask, "Where are the boundaries of legitimate medical experimentation, medical research, and medical treatment? When I was growing up, I was naively taught their there were stages to the scientific quest for knowledge.

- Observation
- Questioning
- Hypotheses
- Research
- Theory
- Experimentation
- Conclusion
- Treatment
- Observation
- Adjustment

Every scientific discovery starts with observation and a fundamental question. For Christopher Columbus, that observation started while sitting at the shore and observing the masts of sailing ships going out past the horizon. He observed that as the ship went further and further out, he saw less and less of its topsail.

Experimentation and observation validated his theory, and he drew a firm and precise conclusion based on all of the work he had done before. Lastly, he set out to find funds that allowed him to circle the Earth to find India.

This is how I learned to develop a scientific idea. Yet when we look at the history of the medical treatment of transsexuals, we just don't see this same level of commitment to scientific study from the men who are responsible for defining the condition.

Hirschfeld observed patients suffering from the condition, but never questioned *why* that they were that way. He simply accepted what they claimed would make them happy, and scheduled experimental surgery in an attempt to give Einer what he said he wanted. Hirschfeld could then prove that his personal beliefs were valid. Benjamin did the same thing when Kinsey's patient stepped into his office. He went from observation to experimental hormones, and then off to Denmark for surgery. Money followed the many of the above steps, but got stuck in the experimental phase, and once he started performing SRS, never returned back to Scientific Method 101 to validate any of his own experiments. Stoller went straight from observation to SRS, skipping all the steps in between and again like the others, never questioned the results of his own work.

I admit to the fact that I am clearly biased on this entire issue. I started out this chapter with one of the worst-case scenarios possible (mea culpa, mea culpa).

The goal of this book is to do just this one thing: By taking an elevated view of this landscape and how we got here, I want all of us, the patient and the practioner, to honestly ask ourselves if this is the road we really want to travel. Is gender confusion a genetic blunder, and is the work of these men truly righteous? Or did they take a wrong turn somewhere and end up harming us, their patients?

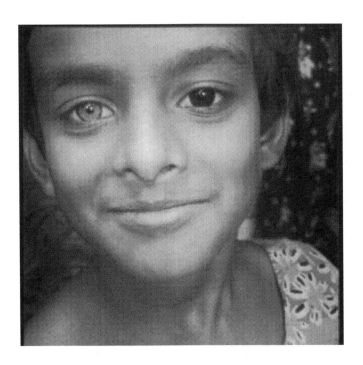

CHAPTER ELEVEN

STANDARDS OF CARE?

As a male who has been under-treatment by doctors for gender dysphoria since 1974, I have been given massive doses of estrogen all of these many years. I had originally lived "as" a woman for 13 years while still having my penis. In 1989, I underwent breast augmentation, and a year later, 1990 went to Colorado for my sex reassignment surgery.

I am not only invested in the outcome of this discussion, I am *fully entitled* to question the medical and psychiatric treatment that I have received over the last forty-plus years

To begin with, let's review what Dr. Harry Benjamin authored:

HARRY BENJAMIN INTERNATIONAL GENDER DYSPHORIA ASSOCIATION'S STANDARDS OF CARE FOR GENDER IDENTITY DISORDERS

The opening chapter states:

"The Purpose of the Standards of Care.

The major purpose of the Standards of Care (SOC) is to articulate this international organization's professional consensus about the psychiatric, psychological, medical, and surgical management of gender identity disorders. Professionals may use this document to understand the parameters within which they may offer assistance to those with these problems. Persons with gender identity disorders, their families, and social institutions may use the SOC as a means to understand the current thinking of professionals. *All readers should be aware of the limitations of knowledge in this area and of the hope that some of the clinical uncertainties will be resolved in the future through scientific investigation.* (author's italics)

The Overarching Treatment Goal; "The general goal of the specific psychotherapeutic, endocrine, or surgical therapies for people with gender identity disorders is lasting personal comfort with the *gendered* self in order to maximize overall psychological well-being and self-fulfillment."

Let's say for the sake of argument that I have just visited a doctor for the first time in an attempt to deal with the confusion I have around being a man. I have been cross-dressing since I was ten. My relationship with my wife of two years is on the rocks because she wants to get pregnant and stay at home and have me support her and our child. I feel tons of pressure over my role as a man, and hate the feeling of having to be the provider, protector, and procurer. Plus I secretly have always wanted to live as a girl. After a year in therapy, I am diagnosed as a real transsexual by my doctor. I eventually make the decision to break up with my wife, and with the doctor's help, begin taking estrogen. My good doctor tells me repeatedly that living as a woman may be challenging and there are social consequences, and that there are side effects to estrogen. My first question is;

Q. Is the hormone treatment I am about to undertake a medical treatment or a medical experiment?

I recall thinking when I popped my first purple pill that I was under a doctor's care. Within weeks of starting hormones, I decide to try going out in public dressed as a "woman". I remember being so afraid that night. I should not have drunk so much Blue Nun wine at dinner that I had to pee, and eventually had to force myself to get up from the table to use the women's bathroom for the very first time. OMG! I worked at De Anza Community College and the restaurant we had chosen was a favorite place of college staffers. The bathroom stalls in there were really short, I was in heels, and my head stuck out over the top while I sat to pee. It was October 9th, 1977. I kept that bottle of Blue Nun for nearly twenty years.

After five years of living full-time as a woman, I asked, and was given approval by my doctor to have the SRS. So here is my question...

Q. Is my sex re-assignment surgery a medical treatment, medical research or a medical experiment?

Well, let's use the Nuremburg Code to guide us.

I. Required is the voluntary, well-informed, understanding consent of the human subject in a full legal capacity.

    A.   Both of these treatments were voluntary. My doctor told me everything he could about the procedures, effects and side effects.

II. The experiment should aim at positive results for society that cannot be procured in some other way.

    A.   Society? Not really, but maybe if I am less miserable, I will ultimately benefit society in some way.

III. It should be based on previous knowledge (such as an expectation derived from animal experiments) that justifies the experiment.

    A.   No, there have been over ten thousand of these types of surgeries on people. No worries here.

IV. The experiment should be set up in a way that avoids unnecessary physical and mental suffering and injuries.

A. Both of my treatments were meant to eliminate pain and suffering, so we are good here.

V. It should not be conducted when there is any reason to believe that a risk of death or disabling injury is implied.

    A. Can't fudge on this one! Cutting off my penis does qualify as a disabling injury

VI. The risks of the experiment should be in proportion to the expected humanitarian benefits.

    A. Absolutely! I will finally live in peace.

VII. Preparations and facilities must be provided that adequately protect the subjects against the experiment's risks.

    A. Not an issue.

VIII. The staff who conduct or take part in the experiment must be fully trained and scientifically qualified.

    A. For the twenty-thousand-dollar price tag, they better be trained.

IX. The human subjects must be free to immediately quit the experiment at any point when they feel physically or mentally unable to continue.

    A. I paid my check and bought the airline ticket of my own free will.

X. Likewise, the medical staff must stop the experiment at any point when they observe that continuation would be dangerous.

    A. Not as chance that I would ever ask them to.

So? What say you? It certainly doesn't look like my gender identity treatment plan of taking hormones and having a sex change fails to meet the standards under the Nuremburg Code for experimentation.

But wait one moment. What about that thing that Dr. Benjamin said… ***All readers should be aware of the limitations of knowledge in this area, and of the hope that some of the clinical uncertainties will be resolved in the future through scientific investigation.***

This statement is coming from the man who created the first sex change clinic in America and wrote a book on transsexuality. And he puts a caveat in the first page of his Standards of Care that clearly tells everyone to be aware of *limitations of knowledge in this area.*

Hello people! I am about to have my penis cut off, and I am trusting that my therapist and doctors know this all of this shit. What does this Dr. Benjamin mean, *"limitations of knowledge in this area'?*

What Dr. Harry Benjamin knew was that his treatment didn't fit the disease! What I have shown you is that all of the medical treatment options for transsexuals, gender dysphoric, cross-gender confused patients (or whatever name you want to call it) doesn't fix the cause of the condition. There is no science *to this science.* You have to look no further than the history to see this.

I. Hirschfeld performed the first SRS experimental surgery on Wegener without ever questioning or trying to resolve his emotional conflict first. It wasn't a treatment, it wasn't research. No, it was a medical experiment worthy of Joseph Mengele,

Karl Brandt and the Third Reich, with surgeons who had not done any previous animal or patient experience performing the surgery, and no previous knowledge of technique or capabilities to implant a human organ.

II. Benjamin, after a brief consultation with Alfred Kinsey, started giving his new wonder drug, estrogen, to a boy patient. Benjamin also had no previous animal or patient experience as to side effects of estrogen on males, and had no previous knowledge of technique or capabilities.

III. Money used the Reiner twins as his personal laboratory to prove his theory on nurture vs. nature. The parents signed a consent form and walked right into the abyss, thinking that Dr. Money must know what he was doing.

Iç. Money also falls into this category of boldly going where no man has gone before. Even after the scandal, the medical profession never censured him, nor took away his license to practice medicine. Money continued to write books and lecture for years after the boy killed himself.

ç. Stoller takes these three doctors' work, and by defining gender as a personal trait, rather than a generic label for social constructs, is able to convince an entire generation of physicians that transsexuality and core gender identity is real.

çI. Pay particular attention to the what he titled his second book! "The Transsexual Experiment," which says a million things about his personal attitude on the subject. He didn't title it "The Cure for Transsexuality," or "The Causative Factors in Children and Gender Confusion."

çII. As a result of Stoller's categorizations of gender, thousands of patients have been mutilated by sex reassignment surgeries after simply signing medical consent forms which follow Nuremburg Code #1.

"Required is the voluntary, well-informed, understanding consent of the human subject in a full legal capacity."

I feel so much better now, I signed a release form. Please doctor, go ahead and cut off my penis.

In the September 15 , 2016 "Today" section of the Singapore Times, there is an article about the medical ethics code for doctors in that country, which was being updated to keep up with the times. After several years of discussion about patient standards of care, the Singapore medical board produced a sixty-six-page document which, after review, is nothing more than the Nuremburg Code 2016 with some thought given to social media. The only really new condition is a "cooling off" period between the patient's consent and the treatment they receive.

In addition, "doctors must take reasonable care to ensure patients do not have psychological or psychiatric illness involving self and body image before performing procedures."

What is gender confusion but, a psychological illness involving self and body image???????

But since there is now such a rabid activism around transsexual rights, the medical profession fearing the Politically Correct Police, has dropped transsexualism from the list of mental illnesses in the Diagnostics and Statistics Manual of Mental Disorders. Also, the World Health Organization has announced it may no longer classify being transgender as a disorder in the International Classification of Diseases (ICD). With the entire medical profession now kowtowing to social media, this mental illness is set to be washed away in the tide of left-wing social acceptance. (So now it's political?) It is now considered by most American doctors to be an untreatable condition by anything other than surgery. Not only don't doctor's want any oversight in the matter, many of the patients don't want to be held back by the lack of understanding of the condition or the lack of ethics. Everyone wants to do what they want, and not be held accountable for the long-range ramifications of their actions.

At this point in my life I don't care about consent forms, the Nuremburg Code, the Hippocratic Oath, or the Standards of Care. What I care about is that the medical profession has gotten to the point of offering sex changes to anyone that states emphatically they are transsexual. In Oregon, the State medical authority allows a person fifteen years of age to have a sex change without parental consent. Further, the State does not require the patient having to undergo any type of psychiatric therapy. Some people are busy trying to be kind and sensitive toward transsexual patients, and competing to show the world how liberal and sympathetic they are for trans-people, that *no one* is questioning how we got here, and whether SRS was ever necessary for this condition. Worse yet, the vast majority of individuals are so desperate to relieve their confusion and torment that they rush like lemmings toward the cliff that is SRS. We're all jumping off this cliff, looking for the panacea of a condition these four men have led us to believe exists.

I, like thousands before and since, made that leap, believing these four men knew this was the right path. There is not one medical nor psychological condition known to man that would allow mutilation and removal of a perfectly functional sex organ for mental/social dysfunctionality. (Bringing up 16-year old rich girls getting tit jobs doesn't cut it folks!)

The dictionary defines experimental procedure:

(1) Not proven by scientific evidence to be effective, or

(2) not accepted by health care professionals as being effective.

Am I wrong in thinking that a medical procedure, after which 47% of patients attempt suicide, is not effective? Would doctors continue performing breast augmentation surgery on young women if 47% of them tried to kill themselves after it, or 47% of rhinoplasty patients? No amount of empathy for what we go through as individuals can justify letting any person undergo these procedures.

Once again, I must bring up the reality of this century-old medical experiment. Let's assume for a moment that Dr. McHugh was the horrible person his critics say he is who accepted his position at John Hopkins with the full intent of ending its sex change clinic. And then he, and somehow convinced Dr. John Meyer to completely slant his report against the practice. However, below are results of a completely different study done not in the US, but in Sweden. The "Long term follow up of transsexual persons undergoing sex reassignment surgery : Cohort study in Sweden" found the following.

"Conclusion: This study found substantially higher rates of overall mortality, death from cardiovascular disease and suicide, suicide attempts, and psychiatric hospitalizations in sex-reassigned transsexual individuals compared to a healthy control population. This highlights that post-surgical transsexuals are a risk group that need long-term psychiatric and somatic follow-up. Even though surgery and hormonal therapy alleviates gender dysphoria, it is apparently not sufficient to remedy the high rates of morbidity and mortality found among transsexual persons."

Here six Swedish highly trained medical professionals state that once a person has SRS, their gender dysphoria goes away. But then a bit of reality starts to creep into the discussion and they say, "But not "sufficient (enough) to remedy" (the patient's anxiety). Well, I have to ask what they hell do you think might be causing the anxiety? The SRS "cured" the gender issue only by removing all future options to fix the real problem in its wake. It is clear that these doctors believe in SRS as a treatment option, but then go onto refuse to admit that their SRS treatment doesn't fix the issue they are trying to solve.

This brings to mind my 2006 Dodge Durango. I bought it at an auction and after the first time I drove it fell in love with the ride and comfort. I've owned a lot of cars in my day, and I confess to being a gear head when it comes to cars and machines. I loved this car. After driving it about two thousand miles I noticed that the temp gauge started creeping up when I was driving around San Francisco. A couple days later, I noticed water dripping under the engine when I got back to my hotel. Sure enough, it was the water pump. I didn't have any tools with me at the time, so $500 dollars later, and new water pump, hoses, blah blah blah. I had my baby back with me for about three weeks when I went up to Oregon on business, and about the time I got to Medford, I started smelling radiator fluid. The Dodge dealership looked at it and said oh it's the radiator. Fine I said, fix it! The day I picked it up, I drove a block and it started smoking from the tail pipe. Back to the dealer. Oh, this time it's a blah blah blah. "Fine, screw it, just fix it!" I yell, being none the lady in my delivery!

Now three weeks, and $3500 later, I'm on the road back to Nevada. Four hours into the trip, and just about the time I get into Weed, California, the engine blows up. The mechanic who later looked at it, said that there was a large crack in the engine cylinder wall that had been there for some time, but all the other mechanics had missed it.

What is the point you ask?

The point is that nothing I could do to fix it, fixed it. No amount of money I could throw at it could fix it. And sex reassignment surgery is just like this, because we are using the wrong tools and wrong parts for something they can't fix with these tools and parts.

When we look at the history of the medical professions' experience with gender dysphoria, we see men trying their best to fix the condition with the tools they had. Some of these men were driven by ego, some by passion, some by curiosity, and some by sympathy.

We see doctors trying to figure out this puzzle that you and I live with every day. All those who have gone before and after us share the same struggle to forget our past and the seemingly unending craziness that makes up our lives.

There is an old saying, "You can't get there from here,"

I present just that logic to all of you. We can't find the peace and quality of life that we want from where the medical profession has taken us over the last century. We can't get there from hormones, cross-dressing, boob jobs, electrolysis, sex changes, and name changes. Gender dysphoric individuals will *never* find peace while living at odds with the entire world.

It is that simple. I want to end this chapter with a short piece that Dr. McHugh wrote. I find no anger and bitterness coming this man. Instead, I find a compassionate and professional doctor that sees the current futility and insanity of how we, as transsexual patients, are being treated by his colleagues. For the life of me, I just can't find the malice that pro-transsexual advocates claim there is.

If Dr. McHugh is harboring any resentment, I believe it is for a medical profession that has failed to protect thousands of emotionally ill patients from themselves and their doctors.

The following excerpt is from *Psychiatric Misadventures* by Dr. Paul R. McHugh

"This interrelationship of cultural antinomianism and a psychiatric misplaced emphasis is seen at its grimmest in the practice known as sex-reassignment surgery. I happen to know about this because Johns Hopkins was one of the places in the United States where this practice was given its start. It was part of my intention, when I arrived in Baltimore in 1975, to help end it. Not uncommonly, a person comes to the clinic and says something like, "As long as I can remember, I've thought I was in the wrong body. True, I've married and had a couple of kids, and I've had a number of homosexual encounters, but always, in the back and now more often in the front of my mind, there's this idea that actually I'm more a woman than a man."

When we ask what he has done about this, the man often says, "I've tried dressing like a woman and feel quite comfortable. I've ever made myself up and gone out in public. I can get away with it because it's all so natural to me. I'm here because all this male equipment is disgusting to me. I want medical help to change my body: hormone treatments, silicone implants, surgical amputation of my genitalia, and the construction of a vagina. Will you do it?" The patient claims it is a torture for him to live as a man, especially now that he has read in the newspapers about the possibility of switching surgically to womanhood. Upon examination, it is not difficult to identify other mental and personality difficulties in him, but he is primarily disquieted because of his intrusive thoughts that his sex is not a settled issue in his life. Experts say that "gender identity," a sense of one's own maleness or femaleness, is complicated. They believe that it will emerge through the step-like features of most complex developmental processes in which nature and nurture combine. They venture that, although their research on those born with genital and hormonal abnormalities may not apply to a person with normal bodily structures, something must have gone wrong in this patient's early and formative life to cause him to feel as he does. Why not help him look more like what he says he feels? Our surgeons can do it. What the hell!

The skills of our plastic surgeons, particularly on the genito-urinary system, are impressive. They were obtained, however, not to treat the gender identity problem, but to repair congenital defects, injuries, and the effects of destructive diseases such as cancer in this region of the body.

That you can get something done doesn't always mean that you should do it. In sex reassignment cases, there are so many problems right at the start. The patient's claim that this has been a lifelong problem is seldom checked with others who have known him since childhood. It seems so intrusive and untrusting to discuss the problem with others, even though they might provide a better gage of the seriousness of the problem, how it emerged, its fluctuations of intensity over time, and its connection with other experiences. When you discuss what the patient means by "feeling like a woman," you often get a sex stereotype in return-- something that woman physicians note immediately is a male caricature of women's attitudes and interests. One of our patients, for example, said that, as a woman, he would be more "invested with being than with doing." It is not obvious how this patient's feeling that he is a woman trapped in a man's body differs from the feeling of a patient with anorexia nervosa that she is obese despite her emaciated, cachectic state. We don't do liposuction on anorexics. Why amputate the genitals of these poor men? Surely, the fault is in the mind not the member. Yet, if you justify augmenting breasts for women who feel under endowed, why not do it and more for the man who wants to be a woman? A plastic surgeon at Johns Hopkins provided the voice of reality for me on this matter based on his practice and his natural awe at the mystery of the body. One day while we were talking about it, he said to me: "Imagine what it's like to get up at dawn and think about spending the day slashing with a knife at perfectly well-formed organs, because you psychiatrists do not understand what is the problem here but hope surgery may do the poor wretch some good." The zeal for this sex-change surgery--perhaps, with the exception of frontal lobotomy, the most radical therapy ever encouraged by twentieth century psychiatrists--did not derive from critical reasoning or thoughtful assessments. These were so faulty that no one holds them up anymore as standards for launching any therapeutic exercise, let alone one so irretrievable as a sex-change operation. The energy came from the fashions of the seventies that invaded the clinic--if you can do it and he wants it, why not do it? It was all tied up with the spirit of doing your thing, following your bliss, an aesthetic that sees diversity as everything and can accept any idea, including that of permanent sex change, as interesting and that views resistance to such ideas as uptight if not oppressive. Moral matters should have some salience here. These include the waste of human resources; the confusions imposed on society where these men/women insist on acceptance, even in athletic competition, with women; the encouragement of the "illusion of technique," which assumes that the body is like a suit of clothes to be hemmed and stitched to style; and, finally, the ghastliness of the mutilated anatomy. But lay these strong moral objections aside and consider only *that this surgical practice has distracted effort from genuine investigations attempting to find out just what has gone wrong for these people--what has, by their testimony, given them years of torment and psychological distress and prompted them to accept these grim and disfiguring surgical procedures".* (author's italics) We need to know how to prevent such sadness, indeed such horror. We have to learn how to manage this condition as a mental disorder when we fail to prevent it. If it depends on child rearing, then let's hear about its inner dynamics so that parents can be taught to guide their children properly. If it is an aspect of confusion tied to homosexuality, we need to understand its nature and exactly how to manage it as a manifestation of serious mental disorder among homosexual individuals. But instead of attempting to learn enough to accomplish these worthy goals, psychiatrists collaborated in an exercise of folly with distressed people during a time when "do your own thing" had something akin to the force of a command. As more physicians and psychiatrists give in to this treatment they abandon the role of protecting patients from their symptoms and become little more than technicians working on behalf of a cultural force." End quote.

I know from my own experience that I was so desperate to stop my own mental suffering that I would have jumped into a tub of boiling bat dung had I been promised it would resolve my CSIC once and for all. It is out of that desperate state that hundreds of people present themselves to doctors every year. And it is out of that same desperation that doctors try all the worn out, and useless tools to fix our broken lives.

Isn't time we look into other approaches to this condition?

CHAPTER TWELVE

THE REALITY OF HUMAN/SEXUAL NATURE
BINARY BEINGS

We now stand looking out at a world created by others. We have traveled far across a vast inhospitable terrain. Our friends and colleagues dropped by the wayside long ago, leaving us to our own journey. CSIC patients are no less guilty for following their route through this wilderness, then they are for leading us down an unknown path. The need to blame others for our predicament ended when our thirst began to be unquenchable. What began long ago as a quest to find self has ended up becoming a quest to save self from self-desire.

I am not asking you to believe my assessment of the facts that I have put forth in the previous chapters. The last thing in the world I would ever wish is for me to become is one of the medical/psychiatric prophets that people follow off a cliff, desperate to find answers to their pain. What I am suggesting is that we all *stop* and assess the path we are on. There is no harm and no foul in taking a break from this path to examine all of the basic assumptions that have developed around this condition. Let us take a new, fresh look at the foundation of ideas, the research that has or needs to be done, let's look at all experiments related to this, at the medication, the surgeries, the treatment plans, and see where we stand.

But, if (and it is a very big "if") this book has given you pause in your quest to find answers for your cross sex identity confusion, then allow me to give you further insights into my core logic.

I have lived a full life. I have had the privilege to have loved and been loved by wonderful people. Prior to my sex change, I had just about every imaginable kind and type of sex you will ever find in a book. I have had sex with hundreds of men and women of various sexual persuasions. I have been intimate and sexual with people who were into S&M, B&D, pedophilia, bestiality; porn makers and watchers; enema givers and takers; women who were into being pissed upon, and men who defecated in baby diapers. I have slept with straight women, straight men, gay men, lesbians, transvestites, transsexuals, bisexuals, and nuns. Having said this, I thought I had zero chance of ever being confused by human sexuality, until one day I was reading a paper and came across the following:

"Transgender man gives birth to his female transgender partner's baby"

This f**ked with my brain in so many ways that I cannot begin to describe. I read this headline and immediately I blew a mental fuse. In the deepest recesses of my soul, this screws with what even I think of as "normal" in my abnormal world. And it continued to do so, until I began digging deeper and deeper into human nature for my book, *It's Who We Are, It's What We Do.* It was then that the woman's story became clear to me.

It was only then that I came upon the simple yet much overlooked realization that humans are a simple, binary sex organism and there is only male and female, with two distinct anatomies. I came to believe this as the *most singular important aspect of our beings* and our CSIC is at odds with our own human nature. When I accepted this simple fact my own life and gender confusion became instantly clear. The Prime Directive of our species is singular in its desire: *"the survival of the species through reproduction."* We are *that* simple. All of the social interactions, tool development, society creation, building of cities, and wars are inconsequential to The Prime Directive. The survival of our species fuels our hormones, our need to have sex, to procreate, to build a safe home for our family, to protect our offspring, and every other "drive" we have as humans.

Anything not related to The Prime Directive means nothing.

Once I had gotten to that point in my thinking, the actions of this female-to-male transsexual became crystal clear. She was after all, an anatomical female. For the female, the only important drive is to get pregnant and to care for the offspring. The fact that she came out of childhood with conflicted thinking around her role in the family is inconsequential to her primary genetic drive. Her need to get pregnant and give birth was still there despite her emotional confusion.

That same drive is in each and every one of us. It will find a way to express itself regardless of any real-world circumstance. In my reading of history, I use to be confused by people who get pregnant in the middle of a war zone. I couldn't imagine how people would want to have sex with bombs falling all around them. But it is because of The Prime Directive that this happens. War, pestilence, starvation, failed crops, tornadoes, and economic downturns have little effect on a human's primary drive to procreate. Women and men want to engage in sex despite all external factors, a fact has been documented over thousands of years.

In our discussion on how best to treat CSIC, we need to look closely at the case of the female-to-male who got pregnant. That drive to get pregnant exists in all of females. Why do you think no physician or psychiatrist has ever offered a remotely valid reason as to why the majority of male-to-female patients continue to be attracted to women, even after hormones and surgery??? Hello, this is so obvious!

It's because they are males who are driven to procreate with females. It is in the male's DNA to be attracted to females. This is not something that we should gloss over. It is so fundamental to this discussion that, unless we give it the full credit it deserves, I fear the research into this mental condition will remain in the dark ages for decades to come.

This drive compels males and females look to each other to fulfill each other's most important need. When a person comes out of childhood confused about their role in the family and in society, they are still males and females. For those medical professionals who believe that transsexuality is caused by some biological factor, I ask you, if this is the case, then why did the person's drive to procreate not modify itself to act in unison with the new failed/changed biological condition?

It makes absolutely no sense (from what we know about biology) for a body to be radically changed by female hormones in-utero without corresponding changes to the entire makeup of the fetal brain. The theory is: The male brain has been grossly modified so significantly by the mother's hormone dump (or whatever guess they come up with) that "he" now believes himself to be a "she". So, my question is, then why did that change also not affect the corresponding sex drive of the fetus's anatomic sex? And why did it not affect the male's desire to mate with and impregnate females, and vise-versa? One popular theory would have us believe that pre-birth hormonal or chromosomal changes are so great as to influence the "gender identity" of the individual. But then we are asked to suspend belief that it would not also influence the object of attraction for that individual whose brain was re-wired.

I believe that the desire of most male-to-female transsexuals to be "lesbians" proves that gender dysphoria stems from social factors in early childhood, and not genetic, biological, and hormonal causes as is suggested by LGBT activists. Therefore, the only way to progress on our own path is to abandon the old ways of thinking that our good doctors have promoted. We must first discard all belief in, and acceptance of, their terminology. We must discard Stoller's theory of Core Gender Identity, which implies that our sense of self can be different from our sex. We must completely abandon John Money's belief that gender is an individual trait, rather than a word representing family/social structure.

For the sake of living in reality, and from this point forward, we must accept ourselves *as* our sex. We are males or females. Having gotten this far, we now must reject Dr. Harry Benjamin's term "transsexual." Males are males, females are females. Simply because Dr. Benjamin's patients wanted to live as the other sex does not mean that people are actually cross-sexed, and can't re-align themselves to their biological gender. In spite of Benjamin's declaration to the contrary, the gender gate never existed, and it was never there to close. He was so blinded by his own belief in his limited tools that he never examined his patients deeply enough to understand this. Speaking of tools, we all need to stop taking the hormones of the opposite sex. We need all of our brain cells fully functioning in order to figure out, and sort out our own confusion. Filling our bodies with these dangerous substances only pushes us farther away from the answers we must find.

Lastly, we must all let go of the idea that there is a simple solution to CSIC. Folks, I have lived with this condition since I was eight years old, a period of fifty-four years. As depressing as it sounds, there is no magic bullet that will cure it. The good news is that it can be cured. The feelings of chaos and confusion can be overcome and replaced with acceptance. The bad news is that sex reassignment surgery doesn't fix a thing. When Magnus Hirschfeld operated on Einer Wegener in 1922, he was offering hope, and had Einer actually survived Hirschfeld's medical experimentation, he would have soon found out what all of us have since discovered: that the sex-change surgery only isolates us more than we already were, while CSIC remains. SRS is not the magic bullet. Plastic surgery and breast implants and electrolysis is *not* the answer to this riddle.

Since our own human nature is so beautifully simple, then how do we get back to the basics of whom we are, and reclaim our identity as binary sexual beings? We do this by throwing away all of their labels, pills and surgeries. This leaves us once again with ourselves. I remember years ago, while I was in therapy with a died-in-the-wool Freudian therapist, that I finally confessed my sense of being a woman trapped in a man's body, he screamed at me, "You are a *man* and *must* accept it! His words cut through me like a knife. He totally disavowed the feelings I had been hiding for fifteen years.

I am not telling you that *you are a man and you must accept it*.

What I am suggesting is that if you are anatomically a female, you should embrace your natural self. If you are a male, you should embrace your maleness. All the surgery and pills in the world aren't going to fix any issue that we who suffering from this condition have. We have to do the very same thing that every good psychiatrist and psychologist recommends: We have to accept the truth of our beings. We are males and we are females. Then we have to begin to dig deep inside our minds to identify where this conflict came from. Whether or not we ever determine when it started doesn't really matter. Every person who has entered therapy over the last half-century comes to this same conclusion in their treatment. It doesn't matter how we got here, only that we are aware of how those past conditions have affected our behavior in the here and now.

"I am not what happened to me, I am what I choose to become."—Carl Jung

So I challenge each of you who are struggling with CSIC and wondering how to deal with the inherent confusion and insecurities from this condition, how do you become the best male you can become? How do you become the best female? How do we incorporate your uniqueness into how you live your lives?

Most of my friends, when asked to describe me, will say that there are men, there are women, and then there is Rene. Over the half-century of living with this condition, I have morphed into a combination of both male and female traits. I am a little gear head, as demonstrated by the story of the Durango, and I am a little overly passionate, as demonstrated by my raging about this subject. I know that at the beginning of this book I stated emphatically that there is no such animal. But the truth is, after a half-century of corrupting my body with hormones and plastic surgery, I walk the undignified line between the two sexes. No one else has to ever become an unwanted third sex like myself.

Use the hormones that God gave you. Use the anatomy that you were born with, and not what you can pay to have.

Being a post-surgical transsexual is not, and never will be, a viable life. This goes back to The Prime Directive, and every human being has that identical drive. Because of it, each sex has the ability to spot compatible mates imprinted deep inside our DNA. Watch a woman you are dining with: She automatically judges every other woman in the restaurant on her ability to land a mate. She is also always scanning the room for the richest, most desirable male to mate with. The same thing happens with men. And built into these simple, automatic drives is the ability of individuals to quickly detect whether another person is a potential mate, or if that person is reproductive competition. We all instinctively know if something is "off" with another person, and for people who have tried to cross the barrier between male and female, there will always be something "off" about them/us. It will never matter if Barak Obama holds your hand at work all day to protect you from the mean world. Transsexuals are not and never will be the same as the biological sex they wish to become, and no amount of hormones and surgery will ever get the individual to fit into the social construct created by our own biology. Because our biology will always betray us, SRS makes us social pariahs in the world we live in. Every day for the rest of our life, we must be on guard against strangers and their reactions to us. This is not about being given a nasty look by the grocery store clerk. I am talking about the need for constant vigilance over the tenor of our voice, how we walk, our mannerisms, and how passive or aggressive our behavior is in social settings. Even if you look like Angelina Jolie, it only takes a split second for the wrong person to recognize you as transsexual and violence to take place.

I have worked in over twenty countries, many of them Muslim countries where Sharia Law is practiced. Out of the 30 countries that follow this law, *they do not tolerate homosexuality on any level*. I have lived full-time as a woman since I was 22 years old and pass as a woman better than 99.99% of other transsexuals. Yet even after forty years, I am always on high alert for the least little odd look or comment from others. Our lives actually depend on it. It is perhaps this level of hyper vigilance that I find the most tiring. The answer is not to attempt to change the laws or the social order so as to circumvent our species biology to support your decision to live as a woman. The answer was back in 1975, when a medical profession should have helped me find the reasons for my fear of living as a male. The answer to CSIC is not attempting to force people to accept my lifestyle by imposing laws and fines in the workplace.

The answer certainly is *not* by changing every bathroom in the United States to accept both sexes. The answer is not by forcing all 330,000,000 Americans into subjugation to my deviant life and lifestyle. If you think that living in a Muslim country is hostile, wait until these forced changes go into effect and the majority of Americans start to resent those of us who dare walk into a bathroom of the wrong biological sex. Lawsuits are a great deterrent for business owners to comply with a transsexuals' lifestyle demands. But I wonder just how many transsexuals will have the absolute shit beat out of them in the meantime. I wonder how many will be followed out to the parking lot and never be seen alive again. For those social justice warriors reading this, please understand I have been witness to anti-gay, anti-TS hate crimes for fifty years. I have seen gay men beaten half to death by Hispanic gang members in the Castro District of San Francisco. I have led anti-gay bashing marches, taught gay self-defense classes, teargas classes, and gay and lesbian handgun safety classes, and none of them has had any effect on the natural biological response of humans to abnormal people (gays, bi, lesbian, trans). What we are up against in our quest for social justice is not social customs, but *biology*, and that biological drive will always win out, regardless of laws in a dusty book.

The answer to our confusion is by first understanding how it started, and then how best to help us accept our own bodies—warts, penis, breasts and all.

So, to begin with, if you are living as the opposite sex, stop. Yeah, I know what it's like to "purge" all of my women's clothes and makeup. That's not what I am suggesting here. Every person struggling with CSIC has got to make a decision about the quality of life they want. Since we can now see the diagnosis these doctors have created is a myth, we must admit that there is no other side to go live on, or go to. The only peace we will ever find is from identifying and confronting the reality of our situation. It starts with dropping all of the cross-sex ideation. It starts with cleansing our bodies of the drugs we've been given. It starts with going back to live our lives without an affectation of the opposite sex. You don't have to throw out all of your clothes and pills. Just put them aside, take a breath, find a therapist who hasn't bought into these doctors' BS. Call around, and question them as if your life depends upon it…because it does. Benjamin believed in hormones and surgery and he forced his viewpoint on thousands of patients. If your new therapist ever suggests hormones or "doing your own thing" and living life any way you want without regard for the rest of society, thank them kindly, tell them to kiss off, and leave. I would also recommend that you avoid any doctor or counselor that states they treat "transsexuals" You are not a transsexual—*transsexuals* don't exist.

Living genuinely, I believe, does not mean having to put on our emotional armor before we turn on the water for our coffee. Living genuinely does not mean living your life without any regard for what others say and think of you. Living genuinely actually entails consideration for others, empathy for other's feelings, and the desire to live as part of a family and social structure. It is in our DNA to want this. Choosing a post operative lifestyle that does not foster and support this is what causes the high suicide rate among transsexuals. It's not just the pain from the confusion we experience, it's the rejection from the security of our social families, and the impossibility of ever finding a mate, which drives us to kill ourselves. I could write an entire book on why no rational person wants to marry a transsexual, and that those who do, have nuts loose somewhere in their personality. I believe that living genuinely can be satisfying to those of us with this condition. We can work through our confusion and not only accept our anatomy, but the lifestyle and choices that come with that anatomy. It is far easier to do this than you would suppose. Deep inside you is the DNA that drives most of our impulses, and if you only listen to them, you will find guidance by how you naturally respond to others, both male and female in social settings.

Pueblo Colorado airport, going home 1990

Before I crossed over, 1974

CHAPTER FOURTEEN

Margret Mahler

Margret Mahler
Born: May 10, 1897
Sopron, Hungary
Died: October 2, 1985
University of Jena 1922

While the men that I have highlighted seemed to go straight from idea to surgery in 5.6 seconds, Margret Mahler did the unthinkable. She thought long and hard about the topic she wanted to study: childhood development. She observed, developed a basic hypothesis, observed again, rethought her original hypothesis, did experimentation, validated or invalidated her original hypothesis, created a core theory about her idea, did more research, performed more observation, changed the conditions in her observation environment to improve her and her team's capacity to observe and to understand what they were observing, and ultimately drew solid conclusions about of all the above. Her focused work on childhood growth and development enabled her to contribute scientifically credible understanding to this field. It is this rigid approach that most first-year family therapists find daunting when reading her books and papers. They are filled with the language of serious psychological research...which they are.

When Mahler, and her colleagues Fred Pine and Anni Bergman, co-authored the 1975 book, *The Psychological Birth of the Human Infant: Symbiosis and Individuation*, they applied every formal and accepted standard for research they knew of at the time. Their work, spanning the previous fifty years, attempted to do the same. When I read Mahler's earliest papers on the subject, she seemed to instinctively understand that in order for her work to pass scientific scrutiny, she had to conduct every aspect of her research with a controlled and methodical rigor. Every step in her sixty years of study was calculated, unlike that of Hirschfeld, Benjamin, and Money, who appear to have accepted CSIC as an unchangeable permanent condition before their first patient's hour was up.

Mahler writes: "Personal development, security, trust, and self-concept are all related to the attachment between the infant and the caregivers and how separation-individuation and how separation from caregivers is conducted and experienced by the infant." While this seems to be an innocuous statement, it is backed up by her six decades of meticulous observation of infants. In *Symbiosis and Individuation,* she states:

"We observed infants alternately melting into, versus stiffening and stemming against, the mother's body. These and other observations gave us insights into the lap baby's earliest boundary formation within symbiosis much before the baby's earliest approach and distancing behaviors in space would occur. Then we were most carefully observing the earliest signs of differentiation:

1. How does a mother carry her child when she arrives?
2. Like a part of herself?
3. Like another human being?
4. Like an inanimate object?
5. How does the young infant react to the mother's taking off his wraps?
6. Once in the room, does the mother separate herself from the child physically and/or emotionally
7. Is there an "invisible bond" between baby and mother even across some physical distance?
8. Does the mother know what is happening to her infant even though he is at some distance from her?
9. How quickly, how readily, and how appropriately does she respond to his needs?

10. Does the child somewhat later in a locomotor fashion seek out his mother and demanding her attention by the more differentiated means now at his disposal?

11. We observed the child's reaction to his peers

12. To adults other than mother (of varying degrees of familiarity to him)

13. The conditions under which he related to, or more or less vigorously rejected, substitutes for his mother.

14. The mother's actual absences from the mother-infant room, especially those that we planned in connection with her weekly interviews, afforded a quasi-experimental separation experience.

15. We studied the child's reaction to the mother's departure

16. His behavior while she was out of the room

17. His response to her return—the phenomena of the reunion—each of these in relation to the progressions and regressions during the separation-individuation process.

18. These were the ones that took place in the presence of the mother: an infant crawling or walking across the room momentarily cannot find his mother's face among the many present;

19. If the mother is inattentive, perhaps simply talking to others, and so on.

20. From very early on, separations of a passive sort, being left instead of leaving

21. If the mother left the room for a moment or two, what was the reaction?

22. Or she left for half an hour or more for an interview with one of the staff

23. Or, when the child was a bit older and had been at the Center for a while, mother might be gone for an entire morning.

24. If the children were able to spend larger amounts of time away from mother with a "teacher" in a nursery-school-like setting.

25. We observed how the infant reacts to the "holding behavior" of his particular mother,

26. later on his straining a bit away from her, as if to have a better look at her and investigating mother (and "other").

27. From around 5 months we had cues to infer boundary formation, thence active separations from his mother.

28. Does he try, when at some distance, to bridge the gap visually, vocally,

29. Or by actively seeking out his mother and demanding her attention by the more differentiated means now at his disposal?

30. Does the mother keep her infant in her arms a great deal?

31. Does she make a gradual transition by taking him slowly to the playpen, for example, and staying with him until he is comfortable, perhaps offering him a toy?

32. Or can't she wait to be rid of him, dumping him into the playpen immediately upon arrival and turning her attention to other things, perhaps her newspaper or conversation, turning to the child to over stimulate him only as her own needs demand it?

This is the kind and depth of research that has never been done with CSIC patients. These are the kinds of questions that needed to be answered long before any doctor performs SRS surgery or dispenses pills to patients. Simply taking a family history and then giving out Estrogen is not the same thing.

Mahler goes on to state: **"From the standpoint of the body image, the shift of predominantly proprioceptive-enteroceptive cathexis toward sensoriperceptive cathexis of the periphery is a major step in development. We did not realize the importance of this shift prior to psychoanalytic studies of early infantile psychosis. We know now that this major shift of cathexis is an essential prerequisite of body-ego formation. Another parallel step is the deflection—by defense formations such as projection—of destructive, unneutralized aggressive energy, beyond the body-self boundaries (cf. Hoffer, 1956). The infant's inner sensations form the core of the self. They seem to remain the central crystallization point of the "feeling of self," around** *which a "sense of identity" will become established* **"** (authors italics) (Greenacre, 1958; Mahler, 1958b; Rose, 1964, 1966).

"The sensoriperceptive organ—the "peripheral rind of the ego," as Freud called it—contributes mainly to the self's demarcation from the object world. The two kinds of intrapsychic structures together form the framework for self-orientation (Spiegel, 1959). "

(I told you her work was hard to chew through…lol)

In lay terms, she states the infant becomes aware of their own body, then goes on to attribute major significance to that event. And in spite of the fact that the infant has an underdeveloped mind (by adult standards) and near-non existent understanding of the world around them, is still having experiences of their worth, relationships with their mother and other siblings, and family dynamics impressed upon their mind.

"Whatever sexual differences may have preexisted in the area of innate ego apparatuses and of early ego modes, they certainly were greatly complicated, and generally compounded, by the effects of the child's discovery of the anatomical sexual difference. This occurred sometimes during the 16 to 17-month period or even earlier, but more often in the twentieth or twenty-first month. The boy's discovery of his own penis usually took place much earlier. The sensory-tactile component of this discovery may even date back into the first year of life (see Roiphe and Galenson, 1972, 1973); but there is uncertainty as to its emotional impact. Around the twelfth to fourteenth month, however, we have observed that the upright position facilitates the visual and sensory-motor exploration of the penis (p. 72). Possibly in combination with a maturational advance in zonal libidinization this led to a greater cathexis of this exquisitely sensuous, pleasure-giving organ. Incidentally, it is hardly noted in psychoanalytic developmental psychology that the discovery of the penis, and particularly the important experience of its involuntary erection and detumescence, parallel the acquisition of voluntary free locomotion of the body. Except for Lofgren (1968), we did not find any reference to the little boy's noticing his highly-cathected organ, his penis, moving (that is, erecting) on its own. This passive experience is probably very important. It would seem that the little boy becomes aware of the involuntary movement of his penis at the same time that he develops mastery of his own body movement in the erect position" (see Mahler, 1968a).

Mahler, Greenacre, Rose, Freud, and Robert Stoller all understood that individual sexual identity is established in this early phase (up to about the end of the third year.) of infancy and continues through early childhood development, I believe it is here that we must begin our archeological dig. It is here, in the complex chemistry of childhood development, where not only the environmental conditions into which the infant is born but also the social fabric and family dynamics, politics and expectations, that must be examined. And if that were not enough, let's add to this stew the fact that these relationships change during the infant's growth. It is this individuation and separation that Mahler was really trying to dissect in her research. But for the sake of our discussion, we simply have to look no further than the fact that, added to the thirty-two interpersonal reactions/relationship listed above, Mahler noticed that sometimes the infant is growing faster "internally" than externally, and sometimes vice-versa. She found that this may cause a disruption in the relationship between the child and the mother, who may not be ready for her infant to show greater independence at that particular stage in their relationship.

Looking at this another way, if each of the thirty-two conditions has an effect on the infant's sense of identity, then the permutations of these interactions is 633402866629732777061622869468118866098964618 28096. But that's not the least of it. Within each of the thirty-two conditions, let's say that there is a range of effects from that issue of zero to twenty, with twenty having the greatest effect on the individual and the mother. So we would have to multiply the 6334028666XXXXXXXXX number by 20 permutations. This explains why the total number of individuals with CSIC in the general population is so very small.

Therein lies the rub, and as many possibilities as this represents, it does not and cannot include the variances between the mother and other family members have on the particular individual child's mental, emotional, and physical state. Each child will probably react differently to the same conditions, resulting in more and more permutations. And this is excluding factors such as race, economics, and mental illness in one or both parents, social unrest, social status, drug addiction, birth defects, and the number of siblings in the family. But the medical profession has not done their collective homework on CSIC patients, and as such have absolutely no understanding of why this condition takes place with any certainty.

Put another way, we know that gold (AU) is a very rare mineral. We know that there are hundreds of types of igneous rocks, which fall into about ten subgroups; metamorphic rock is divided into two main groups with nine subgroups; the sedimentary class is comprised of three main groups with fifteen subgroups. (In order for one particular mineral, like gold, to develop in sedimentary or metamorphic rock, all the necessary conditions and chemicals that make up the gold to be in right time and place. Temperature, pressure, time and chemicals in the surrounding soil all come into play to create that wonderful mineral we are so fond of. The permutations of necessary factors are in the trillions of trillions. If any of these factors is missing, gold won't occur.

It is exactly for these many reasons that the psychological and medical professions are reluctant to pick up their shovels and start digging to find a cure for CSIC. It is much easier to write a script for a few pills, or write a letter approving surgery than look for the factors that created the condition.

CHAPTER THIRTEEN

THE ORIGINATION OF CROSS SEX IDENTITY CONFUSION

SORTING IT ALL OUT

Recently, I managed a project to build the new English station at Al Jazeera News in Doha, Qatar, and had to go behind the presenter's studio to look at all the networking equipment. The front of the racks was all neat, clean and had lovely colored lights all blinking impressively. But when I went to the rear of the racks, I was shocked to see thousands of cables coming from and running off into every direction. Visually it was just too chaotic to make any sense of, and I stood in wonderment at how Al Jazz news actually continued to operate with so much chaos behind the curtain. In that instant, I had a glimpse of what the human mind's wiring must actually look like. Only recently have we had the tools to crack the mysteries of the brain, and learning that it has over 100 billion neurons (nerve cells). Each single neuron can be connected to approximately 10,000 others producing a possibility of about 100 trillion nerve connections. Our brains have more neurons than the galaxy in which we live has planets. In addition, it is 71% water, and 60% of its dry weight is fat. That ultimately means that we do all the amazing things we do with a brain that has a functional area of only 15% of its total mass.

With this in mind, I fully understand the complexity of the task when I suggest that, to cure CSIC, we must examine our childhoods.

My own confusion started when I was about two years old. My family lived in Alamosa, Colorado, and I distinctly remember not liking to play boy games with my male cousins. I preferred to stay with my girl cousins and play house and darn socks. I was too young to articulate these feelings, but I remember a kind of warmth I felt in the house with all the women doing domestic things. By the time I was six, I was able to put the feelings into words, and would fantasize about being married to a man and having a home with him. I was secretly cross dressing in my older sister's clothes by fifth grade, and by the time I was fifteen, I learned from Dr. Benjamin's book I was a transsexual. My life suddenly all made sense…in a very clinical kind of way. Yet when I picture myself during that time, I am struck by the fact that outside the camera frame was a completely messed up family. I was the youngest of three children, and my father had already distanced himself from my mother by the time those photos were taken. We moved back to Alamosa, my mother's home town, in a vain attempt to help her cope with her schizophrenia. It didn't help and she fell deeper into her own mental illness.

My siblings were seven and eight years older than I, and both were struggling with their own identity issues. My sister later told me that it was while we were living there, she had her first sexual experience with one of our cousins at the age of ten. That event affected much of her life as she grew up and had a family of her own. She turned to religion to rid herself of guilt and shame. It is in this moment that I am now able to see beyond the chaos of the thousands of cables in my mental makeup and identify four strands that come from one place and terminate at another. With my mother's inability to recover her sanity to suit my father, we left the small mining town behind and went looking for a safe haven. It was never found, and by the time I was six my father had abandoned the four of us in a Montrose, Colorado, hotel.

Like my mother, I spent night after night crying for my father, and praying to God to save us from the loneliness and destitution that every member of my family felt. Here is another cable in the schema we can now see. Eventually, my mother was able to make enough money working as a waitress for us to take a Greyhound bus back to Denver. The Denver County Welfare Services were much better than those in Montrose and we landed softer than we did two years earlier. Within a year of returning to

Denver, my mother had a complete mental breakdown and was committed to Fort Logan Mental Health Hospital. She would spend the next seven years having electroshock therapy (EST) and getting loaded on pills. I can now see several long batches of wires clearly and the exact devices they are plugged into. By the time I was ten, I'd been repeatedly raped by one of my mother's friends from the hospital. His name was Roger Peters and he had been hospitalized for child molestation. Now I can understand where the majority of the wires are all coming from, and I understand where they plug into the decisions I've made, the feelings I felt, the confusion I had as a child, my thinking that I was a girl, my desire to escape my pain, my self-destructive urges and behaviors. It was all there in the maze of my mind.

Surprisingly, I figured this out two weeks before I left for my surgery.

It was September 1990, and Dr. Stanley Biber had sent me a confirmation letter of my SRS surgery date. It was set for November 15, 1990. I said I wanted to get rid of my penis and be a girl since 1961, and now I had *the day*. But I couldn't shake this uneasy feeling that I was making a mistake. How could I say that I wanted this my entire life, and still have any doubts? By then, I had been living full-time as a woman for thirteen years. How could the SRS not be right for me? So, I tried to analyze my life in a way I had not done in the previous 15 years of therapy. I decided to write out a timeframe that showed my emotional development, with each member of my family represented in their own

184

timeframe. This timeframe was to include all significant events that I could identify and how these events affected the course of our lives. I became obsessed with writing graphic description of everything I could remember about myself and my family. Unable to sleep, I spent every waking hour documenting my life until two weeks before my surgery. I presented it to my therapist on a chart comprised of fifteen landscape pages side-to-side. I even brought adhesive tape to attach it to her office wall. There, in black and white, was my emotional development, a veritable slide show of how little me became big me. As impressed as my therapist was, I don't believe they understood the full significance of what I had done.

As I sat there looking at my life as a bar graph, I came to the complete and unvarnished understanding that my gender confusion was not biological, nor hormonal, nor from messed up DNA. It was absolutely all environmental—it was family.

Biology does, on occasion betray us. But less than three percent of all live births in the United States have defects. Deformities are very rare here, yet the medical industry has built a profitable business practice on the diagnosis of birth defects for pregnant women. Our biology passes the code from one generation to another on how exactly to be male and female. Unless somehow damaged, our offspring's cells are given a complete blueprint for building a human body. You've got to appreciate just how remarkable this is. We have explored our solar system and surrounding galaxy, and not found any life forms similar to our own…*at all*. There is not a single other planet in our very small solar system (5.65 billion miles across) that shows any sign of life. Humans are the only known intelligent life form in this massive space we call home. We as people have become so complacent about our own existence as a life form, most people don't fully appreciate how unique we are in this part of the galaxy. But I assure you that our own biology does not take anything for granted. That force that drives us somehow knows the overwhelming odds against life forming on any planet in the universe. It knows it so completely that is has mastered the ability to pass along our DNA and create a human being. We are talking about German engineering standards on a universal scale. It is these precise standards for creating male and female life that we must have faith in if we are to overcome CSIC.

If you were born male, you have everything you need to live as a male. If you were born female, and you feel confused about your place in the world, trust your own body for it will not betray you. I think a lot of people who are afflicted with CSIC feel hindered by what they see as ridged social roles for their particular sex. This dis-ease is clearly social in nature, rather than biological. I remember feeling this way through most of my childhood and into young adulthood. I felt so confined by being a man, and resented having to live up to the world's standards. Those standards and expectations were made manifest by the obligatory suit and tie. Every day I put on my tie to go to work, I felt like I was tying a noose around my neck. I hated being called "sir" and "mister" by sales clerks. I grew up hating my male anatomy and was ashamed of my own sexual urges.

If life had a voice to speak to us, it would tell us how totally unique and remarkable each of us are. We are not bound by social constraints or customs. As living beings in the void that is the universe we have been given the most singularly amazing opportunity as living beings to expressing our male and female selves however we choose. Fortunately, I have learned (rather too late in life) that what matters is the act of living genuinely as the person I am, not the act of living as a man or woman. Be yourself, for your body knows how to be what that is.

Embrace it, celebrate it, dance around the room hollering and whooping it up.

CHAPTER FIFTEEN

IT STARTS HERE

It starts here, and it starts with one person. It starts with giving the people plagued by these issues the possibility of living a normal life. It starts with debunking all of the old, biased thinking around the issues of gender confusion, transsexuality, core gender identity, the closed gates, and untreatable conditions.

It has already started and it started in Los Angeles, California.

I received a call this year from my friend, I have known her about seven years; she is a certified trainer of hypnosis, neuro-linguistic programming and Time Line Therapy. In her Los Angeles practice, she uses hypnosis and Time Line Therapy (TLT, thank you Tad James company) to help people change fundamental reactions to events in their far, far past.

This technique was developed by Tad James, who defines it as: how you unconsciously store your memories or how you unconsciously know the difference between a memory from the past and a projection of the future. Behavioral change in an individual takes place at an unconscious level. People don't change consciously. The Time Line Therapy® techniques allow you to work at the unconscious level and release the effects of past negative experiences and change "inappropriate" programming in minutes rather than days, months or years.

She and I helped to resolve one CSIC person's confusion, using this exact technique.

By Ms. SZ

"While I was attending a meeting, a man in his late 60s approached me about working with his granddaughter. He explained that she was 18 years old, had Asperger Syndrome and was feeling, as he put it, "in a very dark place." Could I help her, he asked. When I visited their home for the first time, I was welcomed by a young woman of 18 with a very tight hug. It was the man's granddaughter and she stated that she was trusting of me, because, I knew her grandfather and *he* trusted me. She had been raised by him from the time she was 5 1/2 years old.

PATIENT HISTORY: Patient's parents, the grandfather's son and daughter-in-law, were both drug addicts at the time of her birth, and lacked the mental, emotional or financial ability to raise their child. During childhood, the patient developed health issues, due to her mother's drug addiction during pregnancy. In addition to being deaf in one ear, she was born with hydrocephalus –(water on the brain). This meant that she needed a stent in her skull for the first few months of her life to drain the fluid. However, after she overcame hydrocephalus, the girl remembers always being depressed. In addition to her drug addiction, the patient's mother suffered from myriad mental health issues, including paranoia and depression, rendering her incapable of being "present" for her daughter, unable to give her the love required to make her baby girl feel secure and happy. While the father was also a drug addict, he tried to be more present for the girl after she reached the age of two or three. He didn't make enough money to properly support her, and despite his concern for the girl, he was too emotionally stunted to be effective. The patient stated repeatedly that she couldn't rely on her father to ever show up when he said he would, and rationalized his neglect, saying he was tired from working all day. As a result, she grew up feeling alone and unloved. Eventually, the girl's grandparents stepped in and took sole responsibility for raising her. After a few more sessions, in which I gained the girl's deeper trust, she started crying, and told me these were "tears of joy." She said that she now realized, after all these years, that she was very relieved to know that she wasn't responsible for her parent's wellbeing. She couldn't handle her own life, so how was she to make their lives better? A few weeks later, my patient told me she had something on her mind that was really tearing away at her sense of self. She felt comfortable enough to tell me that she was a "trans", explaining that, for most of her life she never felt like a female and didn't want to be a girl. While she was clear that she didn't want to undergo a sex change, she wanted to be addressed by a boy's name. She wasn't sure that she could reveal this to her grandparents, as she was afraid of being thrown out of their home. I told her that I would be happy to help her explain her feelings and concerns to her grandparents, if that would make things easier for her.

We did indeed have a family meeting the following week at their home. She had great difficulty explaining her feelings to the grandparents, and fumbled for words. She wanted to continue using facial make-up to hide her acne, and continue wearing bright red lipstick. She also decided that she wanted to be called "Terry." (I found this interesting in that this is both a male and female name.) Her grandfather lovingly explained that this would make her look like a "freak" to those who observed her in the world, especially if she was going to wear masculine clothes. He asked her why she would want to make her life more difficult in this way, when she was already having difficulties with schoolwork and other aspects of living.

Her response was that she didn't believe gender roles mattered. She felt that she could dress and make herself up in any way she desired, firmly stating that she didn't care what anyone else thought. After this meeting, our sessions focused more on her transsexuality than simply overcoming her dark feelings. Yet I knew they were all tied together.

RESEARCH: It was at this point that I contacted Rene, knowing that she was in the process of writing a book on the subject. (*this book! RJ.*) Being a straight Jewish woman, I had little exposure to the LGBT community in Boston, and didn't fully understood the subject until I spoke to Rene. She explained that the current medical explanations for transsexuality, core gender confusion, and gender were all misconstrued. The only way to progress with this young woman was to strip away the crutches that these labels give people. She further explained that if the patient is offered hormones, cross sex living and SRS for their emotional problems, they will never deal directly with the causative factors behind their confusion.

TREATMENT: Armed with this new knowledge, I began working with the patient on the assumption that this was the only identity and body she had to work with. We needed to understand what these symptoms meant. What became very clear as the treatment progressed was exactly as Rene had stated. My client was really denying her femininity, because of her inability to relate to a mother, who had such serious mental health issues.

During the week between sessions, the girl's grandmother texted me an update, telling me that she had brought her granddaughter to Target to get some new clothes. All the plaid flannel shirts she claimed she wanted at previous sessions were too big for her. So they went over to the "junior" department, where the patient found a pink frilly dress she just had to have. She also bought more makeup.

We met the next week and I did a hypnotic session using Time Line Therapy, using Rene's expert input.

TIME LINE THERAPY: The first thing I did was to place the patient in a hypnotic trance state, where she recognized that she was indeed a female, based on her organs, hormones and chromosomes. Then I had her recognize the fact that there was a great difference between "not being her mother," who represented abuse and neglect, and the need to change her gender role. She was easily able to understand these differences and firmly agreed while in trance.

Next, using TLT, I had her go back in time to when she was at Target with her grandmother, looking at flannel shirts. I asked her to "feel" the feelings she experienced at that moment. She admitted that she didn't feel very good about it. Then I had her go back to when she chose the pink frilly dress. She said she felt very comfortable with that choice, along with the makeup, which gave her a sense of control over her appearance, allowing her to hide her acne and emphasize her lips. Time Line Therapy helped this young woman peg an emotionally positive experience to being a female. That in turn was an emotional trigger that returned time and time again with the act of shopping for female clothes.

I asked her if she felt the need to use the boy's name any longer, especially since her grandparents really couldn't remember to use it after almost 19 years. She said that they could use her given name.

Lastly, I asked her if she could love herself as she was with the beautiful female form she was given, dressing as the female she is, while letting go of the "trans" issue. Could she understand that this really wasn't a "trans" issue, because transgender doesn't really exist? She finally agreed with those statements. I then explained to her that this whole issue was about her own need to claim herself for herself, without a thing to do with her mother, who was not and never would be a real parent. I asked her to feel the liberation of that reality. She sighed with relief.

The patient ultimately agreed that this felt so much better than trying to be someone else. She finally was in touch with her femininity and all that it gave her, including, of course, her beloved trips to the store to purchase makeup. This is something she now does every time she has the opportunity.

CONCLUSIONS: The truth of the matter is that, all too often, emotional states get confused with needless and misinformed labels such as "transgender," when the condition doesn't even exist. As we found out, the true cause of gender confusion in this young woman was from her need to *de-identify* with an abusive and/or neglectful authority figure, claiming in this case, her own identity for herself.

So, there was absolutely no need for damaging sex hormones, body-disfiguring surgeries, or a lifetime of feeling discontent regarding one's gender. We hypnotists are very well aware that, until we get to the true cause of the "presenting problem," (in this case gender dysphoria) we can't really help them. It is not until we help our clients release the presenting problem that they can reclaim their lives. It's always a beautiful thing to witness. It has been six months and the girl reports that she has not fantasized about being a man again. *"

I worked with her for only about three weeks to discuss various aspects of the young woman's obsession with changing her sex. It was clear from the very beginning of their sessions, that the only way for her to get at the causative factors of the patient's problems was to wade deep into the swamp and try to drain it. Any identity confusion has a thousand-thousand related issues, and they are all closely guarded by highly developed emotional defense mechanisms.

I believe that in part, my own personal confusion was, like this young woman, a defense reaction to defend the little boy I was back in 1957.

This picture was taken of me at my uncle's house in Alamosa, Colorado in 1957, and I actually have a memory of that moment. Looking at it, I have to ask how any little kid could defend himself against a world where his father is a violent drunk, and his mother was lost in her own schizophrenic fantasies. How could this little kid, living with so much going on around him, be able to grow up normal? Most children, when faced with adversity, do manage to grow up without too many emotional issues. But the chemistry, the pressure, the temperature and genetics of my life created my identity confusion.

I have personally used Time Line Therapy on several occasions with my own hypnotherapist. In a nutshell, the therapist takes me farther and farther back into my memories until I can identify where I first realized I felt like a girl. In my case, it was while I was in 5th grade. By that time, I was living alone with my mother and she was in a very bad mental state . Between not being able to live the dreams of a normal nine-year-old boy, I was forced by circumstance to be the caregiver for my mentally ill mother while suffering through her mental and physical abuse. My life was a living hell. I became jealous of my older sister, who had left home and was living her own life. It was then that I had the first feelings about wanting to be a girl. Being a man at the young age of nine sucked, and I wanted to escape like my sister Anita did. I wanted to "be" her. I had talked around this issue in regular therapy for fifteen years, and it wasn't until I worked with one of her colleagues that I discovered that feeling. TLT took me back to the situation that triggered my desire for escape.

What is more important is the fact that we now have *one* person who has stepped back from the ideation of being a transsexual—ONE PERSON! It did not take years in therapy, it did not require hormones or surgery. She did not have to get on the plane to go find herself. And if there can be one person, there can be others that can be successfully treated to avoid sexual mutilation that is SRS. This was not electro-shock therapy on any level. What I am suggesting is that professionals and lay people alike try something different rather than setting themselves up for the failure that is SRS.

LET US REVIEW

Bicycles and turnips have gender. Not people. People have one of two sex/anatomies. Characteristics of a group, if displayed across that group are called *stereotypes*, not *gender*. A person may display a wide range of emotional behaviors. Males may be kind, sensitive, and enjoy shopping and decorating. Females may love to get their hands dirty pulling an alternator from their Ford, (which unfortunately for those of us who own Fords, happens more frequently than we would like). Some emotional traits are more predominant in one sex than the other. In each of the above (and all other) scenarios, the outward expression of identity is unrelated to the individual's sex. Cross-sex living, hormones and SRS are not options under any circumstance.

Let's talk about my 2004 Ford F350 for a minute. Just because I keep having problems with the cheap-ass

Mexican-built alternators from O'Reilly's going out on me, doesn't mean that I cut off the rear dully axel, replace it with a ½-ton axel, pull off the truck bed, remove the rear electric window in the cab, and for good measure, drop in another size of engine. No, I fix what is broken. I find another source for alternators. I check the electrical system to ensure something electronic in the truck isn't frying the alternators. Is the serpentine belt in alignment with the pulley on the alternator? What other options do I have to giving my big-ass truck a sex change?

Just as getting down to the real issue with my truck was a real pain in the axe, so is getting down to the real issue with our broken personalities. It took me 25 years to figure out mine CSIC issues, but by then I had fifteen years of hormones, and lived as a woman for 13 years. I had been in transition since I was a sixteen, and just couldn't go another day not being a guy, and only half a woman. I knew two weeks before I left for Trinidad, Colorado, to have my surgery, that I didn't need to have it to live my life. I had figured it out. But after a lifetime of pain from all this shit, I could not go back to living as a man and have to be in transition yet again, this time to the male role. I didn't have it in me on November 1, 1990.

I had no more fight in me. I had given up the love of my family. I had allowed the only woman I have ever truly loved to leave me over my gender issues. I had tolerated her aborting our pregnancy because she didn't want it to be confused by its own father. "How could we explain that to the baby?" she asked.

199

I was the very first transsexual to be sworn in as a police officer. It was June 1980 and I cannot tell you how bad the abuse was from other San Francisco Police officers. By the time I boarded that Greyhound bus in Pueblo, Colorado to meet my destiny, I had fought thirteen long years for my right to have a sex change. By the time the sun broke through the window of the Trinidad hotel room, I had lost everything I ever wanted: I was forever lost to my birth family. I lost the lover that held my heart, as well as to losing the children I wanted so badly to have with her. When I walked into Dr. Biber's office, I had earned the right to take that gurney ride to the surgery suite at the Trinidad hospital. I knew that very day I that I didn't need to have the surgery. But after paying such a ridiculously high price for that ticket, I had to take the ride. No one else ever needs to get sent flowers for failing to find answers to their emotional problems by taking the (sic) easy way out, via gurney in a remote and strange city.

We start here by never going down that dark road on a bus or a plane to a place where we think people can fix us by an external act. We start here by using the tools we now have, along with the newfound understanding of where those who came before us made their mistakes. We start here and now by fighting for our right to be whole and complete the way we are. We start by being willing to fight the good fight, even when we are so terribly exhausted by it. Don't get on the plane! Don't take that late-night bus late to a strange city, believing your pain will be over in a few short hours. The answers to our CSIC issues are here, right where you are reading this. You are the answer—you have been all along. Your body has been telling you who and what you are since day one. It's our strange and broken homes, families, and societies that caused this. Let's find out together. Let's start here by being honest and not taking the easy way out. The sex of our bodies is where we start. Our bodies have the path all mapped out. We don't need Google Maps to find home. Reach down between your legs and hold your genitals. That is home, that is where we start to find our answers and where we will ultimately end up at. We get there through therapy, hypnosis, Time Line Therapy, and by being willing to tackle our deepest feelings, fears and chaos. Healing and finding peace starts with the first step, not the last one into a surgical suite.

 We start here…

CHAPTER SIXTEEN

A WORD TO KIDS

This chapter is for kids looking for answers.

If you are a kid, and think you are in the wrong body, I have written this especially for you.

I was a kid just like you. Long before iPhone and the Internet was around, I began thinking I was a girl trapped in a boy's body. I was born a boy, and was born with a penis. Both of my parents called me Philip. But something happened when I was really young, maybe around the time I was two or three years old. Something in my family broke. I still don't know if it was my father becoming an alcoholic, or my mother having a mental illness, I don't know what broke, but something did. And because I was still really little, that something had an effect on how I thought of myself and what I thought of my own body. I learned to hate my boy's body, hate my own penis, and I wanted nothing to do with growing up to be a man.

If you're a kid and reading this, and are thinking you are a boy, or girl trapped in the wrong body, then you know what I am talking about.

By the time I was six or seven, I would have fantasies about growing up to be a girl and getting married to a man that would take care of me. I wanted a home, and children by this man who worked and came home to take care of me and our family. In my mind, I wanted to be taken care of. I wanted someone to care for me, and thought the only way I could have it was to be a girl and get married to another man.

I began dressing in my mother's clothes when I was about eight years old. I spent most of my free time dreaming about being away from my own mother and family.

So, you see, you are not alone in having feelings like this.

I eventually left home when I was 17, and started living full time as a girl, even though I still had my male penis. I found doctors that gave me female hormones and when I saved enough money, I had breast implants. After a few more years, I went and had a sex change. That was now 28 years ago.

I tell you this, because I am now an adult. And I understand a lot of things now that I couldn't when I was at your age. Things that the doctors didn't know, or didn't tell me. Things that even my best friends didn't understand enough about to tell me.

What you need to hear from me, because I have done what you're now thinking on doing, is that with few exceptions, the hurt and pain and confusion that you are now going through around not liking your body, will eventually go away.

Before you were born, your body grew and grew and grew in your mother's womb. Then if you look back at your baby pictures, you will see just how little you were when you popped out of your mom. Now look at your body today. You weigh ten times the weight you did when you were born. You are sixty inches longer in height then you were as an infant. Your nose was a flat stubbly little thing, and now is taking shape on your face. Your hair has grown every day of your life since your birthday, and will continue to grow until the day you die.

Growth is what your body is all about.

And that growth is not limited to your body. Your mind is still in the process of growing. You learn every day something new, something to help your life in this world. The chaos and confusion you feel about your body right now, is just a phase you are going through. You will grow out of it. But you will hurt yourself, if you start taking cross sex hormones, puberty blockers, and thinking that you can live in the opposite sex.

Take it from a person who has done this. The sex change surgery will not fix the emotional confusion and pain you are going through. It won't. The only thing that will fix it, is for you to allow your body and mind you were born with to continue growing and maturing, without the toxic medicines doctors want to give transsexuals to transition to the other sex.

And hear me on this, living in the role of the opposite sex doesn't really work on a practical level. Few people outside of the gay and transgender community, really want transgender people in relationships, or in friendships or even at their work. We make them think and feel too much, and our being around is uncomfortable for them. They think we are silly and weird. Few people are willing to look past our appearance to really see us. But if you continue to live as the sex you were born as, you will grow into a place of peace with other people and not be at odds with the rest of the world. This is the way your life should be, not trying to convince everyone that you meet, that you're not weird. I have spent over 40 years cross living as a trans-woman, and have lived and worked all over the world.

Being a man living as a woman, (and vice-versa) just does not work.

But don't let my words make you think things for you are hopeless. They're not. You can live a normal, happy life. You do that by understanding that you and every kid you know, is going through the same process of trying to understand their body, their mind, their role and their place in the world. Just like you are now going through right now.

The first thing you have to do, is reach out to your parents. Tell them to put down their phones and stop surfing the net. Tell them how you feel about your body. Tell them about your dreams of being someone else, of having a different body. Ask them to help you. I know how hard talking to parents can be. My dad was drunk all the time and missing in action the rest of my childhood. My mom was in her own little mental world. But I had plenty of uncles and aunts that I could have reached out to. I had a much older brother I should have told my feelings about. I guess I was too embarrassed by my feelings to say something to him at the time.

The first thing for you to do, is to get parents and adults involved to help you out of this rough time in your life. This confusion will only end if you talk about it to adults.

Secondly, don't fool yourself into thinking that taking the cross-sex hormones and SRS surgery will fix your pain. It doesn't. The only way for your pain and confusion to go away is for you grow up some more, and to understand where it came from, what started it, and find ways to operate in the world with this special part of yourself.

Third, give yourself time to grow up naturally, without cross sex hormones and puberty blockers. With the help of all of your parents and family, you will grow out of this.

Forth, try to stop the day dreaming about living as the opposite sex, and constant focusing on your body. Go out and exercise, go running, go to the gym by yourself. You may not understand who you are, but your body does. Your body has billions of DNA cells that has no confusion about its sex, and it wants to grow and express itself as the sex it was born as. Let it, get out of your mother's and brother's closet and go for a long run. Do it every day. Go swimming, and hiking at every chance you get. If you are a boy, hang out with other boys. If you are a girl, hang out with them. Your body will guide you out of your confusion sooner than you think. Your body knows and will show you the way out of your confusion, and it will do it without makeup, chest wrapping, high heels, or pills.

I wish someone had told me this when I was your age.

I hope these words will help you.

Rene

CHAPTER SEVENTEEN

<u>A WORD TO PARENTS</u>

Every day I have parents and family members of people confused by their gender, reach out to me asking for help in dealing with this issue. On a recent trip where I was on a speaking engagement, I had a dozen different families approach me, many saying that the only support they could find for families was entirely pro-sex change surgery. While there are now countless pro-transgender support groups across the US, there are very few resources for families whose thinking is not in line with the LGBT thought police. We all recognize that it is a good idea for people suffering from this condition to have their family support. But the PC police would have those family members, who haven't drunk their cool-aid, crucified and ridiculed for maintaining their own personal, religious, and fact-based beliefs in the matter. When it comes to transgender politics in 2018, it's the LGBT way or the highway.

So, if a member of your family is struggling with CSIC, how can you support your loved one, while still maintaining your own faith and values?

Only ten years ago, before transgender was weaponized by the left, and sanctioned by both the APA, and AMA there were only about eight surgeries done each month. In 2016 there were over 3,500 people who had sex changes in the USA. This number looks to double every year for the foreseeable future. Individuals suffering from CSIC is in epidemic proportions in the US, UK and EU. Yet our friends at the APA and AMA refuse to mention or talk about this fact. Combined with the intentional attack and destruction of the Western family structure, these medical associations can be thanked for their part in this horrible trend.

Thank G*D I am not a trained doctor, or else I might have drunk the cool aid. So here is my non-doctor, non-therapist advice, take it with a generous helping of salt.

As a parent of an *adult child* who has confusion about their body and social role, be sincere and honest. Tell the CSIC family member that you still love them. They need to hear this. Tell them that you fully support their journey through this painful time.

If the idea of them cross-living is against your beliefs, tell them so and why. This is no time to lie to them and sit back quietly while your kid's life goes to hell. Tell them that your values and religious faith are non-negotiable. Tell them that while you support their continued happiness in life, that you believe they are going down a path that you do not, can not support. You say this out of respect for them as an adult. Loving a person does not mean that you don't warn your kids of dangers. If they had fallen victim to drugs or drinking, no one would question a "hard love" approach to the issue.

Since LGBT activists have now linked their aggressive ideology, with mandatory parental and legislative "support" for the CSIC person, they would have you believe that there is no longer a way to have values that are contrary to their ideology, and still be a decent and supportive parent.

I personally believe that it is up to the parents to be the adult in this relationship. Someone, hopefully you, must maintain a firm grasp of what is real.

Male and female is real. Males are born with male anatomy, females with female anatomy. Binary sex is real.

Non-binary lifestyles, males giving birth, and All-Gender bathrooms is pure LGBT fantasy.

Given the current LGBT mentality, it will be next to impossible to find a doctor that is not in line with this thinking. If you need a good mental health professional resource contact me, renejaxiwritebooks@gmail.com

Secondly and more importantly, if your child still lives with you, and has expressed the feeling that they are CSIC, then the very first thing to remember is that they "aren't girls trapped in boy's bodies" They are simply confused by their feelings around social roles within your family. Support the child's intellectual exploration of the issue, but don't pretend for one moment that they are actually trapped in the wrong body.

And please don't go to a gender doctor. Because the first thing that doctor or social worker will want you to do, is allow the child to cross dress full time, go to school dressed in the opposite role, and be given puberty blockers.

This is the absolutely the wrong thing to do. All research has shown that 95% of children who are CSIC in childhood grow out of that confusion. Yet, 100% of the children who are given puberty blockers are now seen going onto sex changes.

The other thing that is vital for you as parents to do, is look at your own part in the child's role confusion. Dig deep, and be honest with yourself. During the first three-four years of your child's life, what were your own attitudes about this child's role in the family? What was the environment that you created for the child? What was your husband's or wife's attitude toward the child? What were the "truths" that you said over and over to their tiny sleeping ears, that you showed them "the truth," of their place in your life, and in the family?

If you are a mother who was overly protective of your son, and didn't want them to grow up, you have to be honest with yourself in order to help your child. People are either running away from something, or toward something. Is your child trying to run away from some hurting influence in your relationships to him or her, or are they running toward love and acceptance that you won't or can't give them? Where do you and the other family members fit into this cycle?

Knowing this might not affect the outcome of their CSIC, but it might help you not continue poisoning them to believe in their own identity confusion.

Whilst you don't have to suddenly be an ogre about their wanting to wear boy's boots, or nail polish. Don't encourage them to cross dress, don't buy them cross sex toys or clothing. Always support the child's natural anatomy, and then reinforce the fact that "play time is over" and now *is time for them to be their natural self.* At this point in their lives, the greatest gift you can give a child who is believing they are of the other "gender' is your time and to see them as the sex they are born with. Male children need to spend quality time with their fathers. Female children need that special one-on-one time with their mothers. Children learn from seeing and doing and it is up to you, the parent to be their appropriate role model. Put down the smart phones at dinner and engage with them. Get them off the TV, and Internet, and engage. They learn to identify themselves as men, from other men. Girls learn to identify as women by being in rapport with other women. If they are rejecting their social role, then what is the message they are getting from the family, and from you the parent?

As the adult in this relationship, you will most likely have to do battle with your child's school, school nurse and gender doctors. This will be your most important stand for reality. They will all want you to support your child by drinking the cool aid. I've had parents tell me that the child's school is actually taking them to court to get a warrant to keep the parent from talking reality to their children. One woman only found out that her 14-year-old daughter had been prescribed Testosterone by a school doctor, unbeknownst to the parents, when she was putting clean clothes in her daughter's dresser and discovered the drug bottle and needles.

There is a war on reality, and our children are being pitted against parents in their own home. The only way to put an end to this for the parent to remove the child from that school and is do home schooling, or find an oasis of sanity in another school. I am afraid that even the Catholic schools and colleges are now home to the

LGBT movement and protest against all who have drank their hallucinogenic drink.

Recently, I had an older couple approach me about their 25-year-old son, who after attending college began cross living as a woman. He was threatening self-harm unless they began using her (sic) "proper" pronouns. In a letter he sent to the parents, he ranted about G*D is "a vengeful being who is responsible for genocide and mass killings throughout history." He put this into the email, knowing how deeply religious both of his parents are. In his five-page email they shared with me, he even went so far as to blame President Trump for his not feeling safe, and the possibility that he might commit suicide out of fear of his/her safety.

This was not so much a letter asking for their support, as it was a ransom note. In it, page after page he was demanding emotional payment from them or the hostage would be killed. In this case, the CSIC child and the kidnapper where one and the same.

After speaking with me at length about this, the father sent a simple, non-emotional response.

"Our faith and beliefs are non-negotiable."

The parents clearly still love their son, but he was pitting them against all they knew to be right and moral. He was pitting them against their God and everything they know to be real in the world.

My question is simple. Would a rational, mature person threaten suicide and demand their religious parents to stop believing in G*D, all just to be called by a female pro-noun?

It's not that this family doesn't still love him. But unlike their CDIC son, the family is still in touch with reality. The mother and father have not been exposed to the LGBT transsexual ideology while at college for five years, and through the media, college councilors, all gender bathrooms, and bought into the fallacy behind the current transsexual ideology. The parents are still open to having their son be part of the family. But their deeply held beliefs don't allow them to support the cross dressing, hormones, or his homosexual boyfriend. There is a large gap here between what they see as right and moral, and what their son and his school councilor see as a medical necessity. The parents took a wide step toward reconciliation with their child over that gap by drawing their own boundaries on the issue. That is the mature way adults handle conflicts, not in threats of self-harm and ultimatums.

And it may not be ideal for everyone. But that is what rational debate is about. Compromise happens every day in the real world. Sometimes people have to step away from the table, if the terms of the final contract is not in their best interest to continue with the negotiations.

LGBT activists would have us believe that a Win-Win for all sides in this argument is simply for all to believe as they do.

Their son can always go home, and be part of his family again. But just as I am advocating in this book to stop believing in the fantasies that modern medicine has created, it is also up to the CSIC person to come back home to reality. They have to stop believing in the lies that Hirschfeld, Benjamin, Money and Stoller created around the idea of gender can be different from anatomy.

In a world of ever increasing chaos and disorder, home has to be a solid foundation from which the child learns about life and their place in it. But it must also serve the child's journey through adulthood. It must serve as a sanctuary where the returning adult child can return and revitalize themselves and remember what is good, what is right, what is moral, and what is normal.

Anything less than this, turns the parent's home into nothing more than a public laundry, a cheap meal, and a free babysitter service.

CHAPTER EIGHTEEN

REASONS TO NOT GET ON THE PLANE

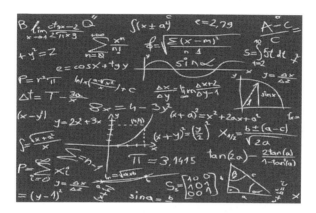

1. Over 40% of all post-SRS surgical patients attempt suicide.
2. Ten percent of those will die from their attempt.
3. Turnips have gender, humans don't
4. Gender is a definition of a group, not an individual personality trait.
5. Humans have anatomical sex, not gender.
6. Transsexualism, core gender identity, and gender dysphoria are concepts created by three men to describe observed behavior in their patients. That does not mean these concepts exist de facto.
7. Sex reassignment surgery is entirely experimental, and not a proven treatment to cure the condition.
8. Personality disorders are hard-wired in the brain, and thus can't be resolved by traditional

psychoanalysis any more than schizophrenia can be.

9. Mutilating your physical anatomy cannot solve a mental illness.

10. The majority of post-operative TS retain their attraction to the opposite sex, as programmed by their DNA.

11. There will always be people who are able to "read" you, no matter how good at passing you are. It is in their/our DNA to do this.

12. Our choices to mate are biologically driven, not socially engineered.

13. Many post-operative SRS persons are forced into the sex industry (prostitution) due to their very limited acceptance into society. (We all can't live in the Castro district of San Francisco, darling!)

14. Hirschfeld, Benjamin, Money, and Stoller never tried to find ways to cure the condition, only study and profit from it.

15. There is a vast difference between medical theory, research, experimentation and treatment.

16. An "informed consent" release form is the only thing that separates Frankenstein experimentation from "legitimate" medical treatment.

17. The only known successful treatment for persons suffering from gender dysphoria/transsexualism is described in the previous chapter.

18. Out of 197 countries on Earth, only the United States offers any civil rights and legal protection to transsexuals.

19. That means there are 196 countries, i.e., *the rest of the world*, where people attempting to live as the opposite sex are at risk for arrest, attacks, and death.
20. 99.99% of the U.S. population is forced into accepting transsexual individuals, even through legislation will not stop people from thinking of you as a freak.
21. SRS surgery never resolves the fundamental mental conflict, the confusion or the pain.
22. Living in the role of the opposite sex alienates the person in crisis from the one thing they need the most: social acceptance and the love and support of family and friends.
23. Long-term and emotionally healthy intimate relationships of post-operative TS are so rare as to be nonexistent. (This and income disparity are leading causes of suicide attempts.)
24. Our bodies are simply not designed to take the hormones of the opposite sex. These drugs are dangerous and cause additional physical and mental stability issues.
25. There is no here - here. Once you have the surgery, medicine has no more tricks up its sleeve to fix the constant knowledge that you are different from all others.
26. Once you fly home, that's it! You are left with the same confusion, the same challenges in relating to people, the same feelings of inferiority and of being different that you had before

spending twenty-thousand dollars to have your dick cut off.

27. Living in the opposite role of your anatomic sex is not a viable lifestyle because of the above reasons.

28. A sex change does not make you the opposite sex. All emotional relief you get from it quickly erodes and you are back where you have always been. (Everywhere you go, there you are!)

29. We have been led down a blind path to these wretched experiments by men who were mortal, and therefore flawed by their limited focus and personal demons.

30. Don't believe the LGBT hype that this is a life saving surgery. If it were so, then why do 50% of TS who have the surgery try to kill themselves?

31. Don't take comfort in the fact that the APA, AMA and a dozen other medical associations have a consensus of opinion, that SRS is right for you. They stand to make billion$$$$$$ of dollars cutting off parts of your anatomy.

32. Ask yourself, why is it that this one surgery, is the only medical condition where doctors _don't_ try to return the injured patient _back_ to their original and natural state of health?

33. Take notice! I have traveled down this path and it is a dead end. Turn back now!

CHAPTER NINETEEN

<u>CONCLUSION</u>

Writing this book has been one of the most difficult task of my life. Having started with a simple core belief that both mental and medical profession had somehow failed me, I undertook to examine and explain how we got here. To do this, I had to transverse a terrain I have known since childhood, but was reluctant to re-examine for the sake of letting sleeping dogs lie. But at some point, I was bound by logic and reason to attempt to put all of my experience into some perspective in this book.

As sanctimonious an ass as I come across in parts of this book, it comes from years of trying to hold back my anger and rage at the outcome of my own life. I must ask you, the reader, for forgiveness when my own personal anger gets in the way of presenting the facts... (as I see them.)

All of the traits I most pride myself for having— intelligence, adaptability, loyalty and stamina—have only kept my rage and sadness shrouded at arm's length these many years. Alas, I have never truly been able to bridle them. Both of these heartfelt reactions to my own mental illness came out at times while writing these pages. Although I have encouraged professional and lay persons reading this to face their own demons stemming from this ailment, I have spent many hours cringing at the thought of doing this for myself in order to present this information.

What I am left with after all of this research and introspection is that despite my generalized anger at the medical profession, it is still here in its infancy.

After personal correspondence over the last year with several of the doctors who worked alongside Drs. Benjamin, Money, and Stoller, I now know that there was solid resistance and outrage from some of their colleagues at their methods and madness. But like any other person and profession, these doctors were too busy with their own practices, and their own lives to spend the time and energy to put an end to the horrific medical treatments being practiced on CSIC patients. And given how little we know of what causes this condition, it is no surprise that one doctor's best guess is as good a treatment, as none at all.

We can only wish that moving forward from this point in time that all medical professionals challenge the brutality and insanity of similar medical experiments upon CSIC patients, regardless of their rationale behind them. Giving free rein to the Walter Freemans of the medical world to roam the country, is just as bad as allowing Money or Hirschfeld to play God with patient's lives without any challenge, oversight or consequence. The APA and AMA continue to dance around the ridiculous high suicide rate of post-operative transsexuals with their flawed illogic and wanton disregard for the lives of the patients whom they continue to destroy with their politically correct self-diagnosis, and surgery approval.

As Stoller so rightly pointed out, the lives of transsexuals are of little consequence to society. We pose little threat (other than the demise of our own potential) and have no social significance per se. There is little reason for anyone in the medical or psychological fields to focus on finding a cure for our confusion and despair.

Yet it is exactly Stoller's arrogant pronouncement in the preface of *Volume Two* that forces a scream out of me every time I read it. CSIC people want love, we want community, we want families, we want companionship, and yes, we want peace. And regardless of how our identity confusion manifests itself, we have the same right to those most basic of human desires as any other person. But while I know the sting of family rejection all too well, I still advocate in these pages for the family to avoid supporting the delusion that a person can be of one body and another, different mental gender. There has to be a sanctuary for the CSIC person to come back to where the pressures the person feels under can be pushed aside for a little bit while the person tries to sort out their feelings. And that sanctuary has to be reality of the family they were born into. It can't be the all of the doctors, surgeons, pharmacists, family councilors and gender clinics who profit from their delusion. How can any person rightly trust any gender doctor who stands to benefit financially from your own pain and confusion? There is not one single instance in medical history where a person has found inner peace at the end of a scalpel.

But this peace can't be achieved through pills or electrolysis and surgery, but it can be identified and achieved through new therapy alternatives. Not one of our desires for communion within the world of people can be obtained by signing a medical release form for an experimental surgery that then pushes us to the fringe of society we see relations with.

Our lives can only be made whole again by first accepting the reality of our human sex, and by no longer looking toward antiquated and disfiguring medical terminology and Nazi-like experiments resulting from the ignorance and naivete of the last century.

Whether you are a doctor or lay person reading this matters not. The only thing that matters is that we stop the sexual mutilation that came to us from our past ignorance and hubris.

If after reading this, you disagree with my assumptions, then please in the name of God most holy, **DISPROVE ME.** Do it scientifically and follow the same rigid methodologies as Mahler would. Follow every ethical and moral guideline you can, and if that is not enough, make up some new ones to avoid the hubris of the Amercian Medical Association and Dr. Walter Freeman. Do the medical research on this subject that it deserves. And work to avoid the pitfalls that the men written about here fell into. Prove me wrong or prove me right, and do everyone suffering from this condition the greatest service possible.

Give us hope where there is now only despair.

Good luck and God speed on your journeys.

Rene Jax.

END

APPENDIX A

NURMENBERG MEDICAL CODE OF ETHICS

- Required is the voluntary, well-informed, understanding consent of the human subject in a full legal capacity.

- The experiment should aim at positive results for society that cannot be procured in some other way.

- It should be based on previous knowledge (like, an expectation derived from animal experiments) that justifies the experiment.

- The experiment should be set up in a way that avoids unnecessary physical and mental suffering and injuries.

- It should not be conducted when there is any reason to believe that it implies a risk of death or disabling injury.

- The risks of the experiment should be in proportion to (that is, not exceed) the expected humanitarian benefits.

- Preparations and facilities must be provided that adequately protect the subjects against the experiment's risks.

- The staff who conduct or take part in the experiment must be fully trained and scientifically qualified.

- The human subjects must be free to immediately quit the experiment at any point when they feel physically or mentally unable to go on.

- Likewise, the medical staff must stop the experiment at any point when they observe that continuation would be dangerous.

REFERENCES

1. Benjamin, H.
    a. (1966). The Transsexual Phenomenon. New York, The Julian Press, Inc.
    b. Prostitution and morality
    c. In time we must accept
    d. Nature and management of transsexualism
2. Bolin, A.
    a. (1987). In Search of Eve: Transsexual Rites of Passage. South Hadley, MA., Bergin & Garvey.
3. Bolin, A.
    a. (1997). Transforming Transvestism and Transsexualism: Polarity, Politics, and Gender. Gender Blending. B. Bullough, V. L. Bullough and J. Elias. Amherst, New York, Prometheus Books:
4. Bullough, B., V. L. Bullough, et al., Eds.
    a. (1997). Gender Blending. Amherst, New York, Prometheus Books.
5. Page 25, * as defined by Dr. Bill Cloke.
6. Case, M. A.
    a. (1995). "Disaggregating Gender from Sex and Sexual Orientation: The effeminate man in the Law and Feminist Jurisprudence." 105 Yale
7. Cohen-Kettenis, P. T.

a. (2001). "Gender Identity Disorder in DSM." Journal of American Academy of Child and Adolescent Psychiatry.

8. Paisley Currah

    a. The State We're in 2008

9. Denny, D.

    a. (2000). "Virginia's Ordeal: S.P.I.C.E. Organizers should be ashamed." Transgender Tapestry 2000

10. Diamond, M.

    a. (1976). Human sexual development: biological foundation for social development. Human Sexuality in Four Perspectives. F. A. Beach, The John Hopkins Press:

    b. (1979). Sexual Identity and Sex Roles. The Frontiers of Sex Research. V. Bullough. Buffalo, N.Y., Prometheus:

    c. . (1993). Some Genetic Considerations in the Development of Sexual Orientation. The Development of Sex Differences and Similarities in Behaviour. M. Haug, R. E. Whalen, C. Aron and K. L. Olsen. Dordrecht/Boston/London, Kluwer Academic Publishers.

    d. (1994). Sexuality: Orientation and Identity. Encyclopedia of Psychology. R. J. Corsini. New York, John Wiley & Sons.

    e. (1995). Biological Aspects of Sexual Orientation and Identity. The Psychology of Sexual Orientation, Behavior and Identity: A Handbook. L. Diamant and R. McAnulty. Westport, Connecticut, Greenwood Press:.

f. (1996). "Self-Testing Among Transsexuals: A check on Sexual Identity." Journal of Psychology & Human Sexuality.

g. (1997). "Sexual Identity and Sexual Orientation in Children With Traumatized or Ambiguous Genitalia." Journal of Sex Research 34(2 (May):

h. (1998). "Intersexuality: Recommendations for Management." Archives of Sexual Behavior

i. (1999). "Pediatric Management of Ambiguous and Traumatized Genitalia." The Journal of Urology

11. Diamond, M. and H. K. Sigmundson

a. (1997a). "Sex Reassignment at Birth: Long Term Review and Clinical Implications." Archives of Pediatrics and Adolescent Medicine

b. "Management of intersexuality: guidelines for dealing with persons with ambiguous genitalia." Archives of Pediatrics and Adolescent Medicine 151(Oct.): 1046-1050.

12. Doctor, R. F.

a. (1990). Transvestites and Transsexuals: Toward a Theory of Cross-Gender Behavior. New York, Plenum Press.

13. Dreger, A. D.
   a. (1998). Hermaphrodites and the Medical Invention of Sex. Cambridge, Mass, Harvard University Press.

14. DRESCHER, Jack MD
   a. (2010) Transsexualism, Gender Identity Disorder and the DSM

15. Ekins, R. and D. King
   a. (1999). "Towards a sociology of transgendered bodies." The Sociological Review

16. Ekins, R. and D. King
   a. (2001). Tales of the unexpected: exploring transgender diversity through personal narrative. Unseen Genders: Beyond the Binaries. R. Haynes and T. McKenna. New York, Peter Lang:

17. Frances, A., H. A. Pincus, et al., Eds.
   a. (1994). DSM-IV (Diagnostic and Statistical Manual of Mental Disorders). Washington, D.C., American Psychiatric Association.

18. Freud, Sigmond.
   a. Civilization and Its Discontents,
   b. The Ego and the Id,
   c. The Future of an Illusion,
   d. Group Psychology and the Analysis of the Ego, The History of the Psychoanalytic Movement
   e. The Interpretation of Dreams

    f. Introduction to Psychoanalysis

    g. Moses and Monotheism

    h. On Aphasia, On Narcissism,

    i. The Psychopathology of Everyday Life

    j. The Question of Lay Analysis, Studies on Hysteria

19. Foucault, M.

    a. (1980). The history of sexuality: An introduction. New York, Viking.

20. Gagnon, J. H. and W. Simon

    a. (1973). Sexual Conduct: The Social Origins of Human Sexuality. Chicago, Aldine.

21. Green, R.

    a. (1987). The "Sissy Boy Syndrome" and the Development of Homosexuality. New Haven and London, Yale University Press.

22. Green, R. and J. Money

    a. (1969). Transsexualism and Sex Reassignment. Baltimore, MD, The John Hopkins Press.

23. Gershman Harry Dr.

    a. 1967 *The Evolution of Gender Identity*

24. Hirschfeld, M. (1910/1991).

    a. Sappho and Socrates (1896)

    b. *The Transvestites: The Erotic Drive to Cross-Dress* (1910), Prometheus Books;

   c. *Homosexuality of Men and Women* (1914) translated by Michael A. Lombardi-Nash, 2000

   d. *The Sexual History of the World War* (1930), New York City, Panurge Press, 1934

   e. *Men and Women: The World Journey of a Sexologist* (1933); translated by O. P. Green (New York City: G. P. Putnam's Sons, 1935).

   f. *Sex in Human Relationships,* London, John Lane The Bodley Head, 1935

25. *Racism* (1938), translated by Eden and Cedar Paul.

26. Ihlenfeld

   a. *Transgender Subjectivities: A Clinician's Guide,*

27. Issay, R. (1997)

   a. "Remove gender identity disorder in DSM." Psychiatric News

28. J.E.B. (1994). J.E.B. v. Alabama,

29. Kessler, S. J.

   a. (1998). Lessons from the Intersexed. New Brunswick, NJ, Rutgers University Press.

30. Kipnis, K. and M. Diamond

   a. (1998). "Pediatric Ethics and the Surgical Assignment of Sex." The Journal of Clinical Ethics

31. Mahler, Margaret S

    a. Of The Human Infant Symbiosis And Individuation Basic Books. Kindle Edition.

    b. The selected papers of Margaret Mahler.

    c. Menvielle, E. J. (1998). "Gender Identity Disorder (letter)." Journal of the American Academy of Child and Adolescent Psychiatry.

    d. *The Destroying Angel: Sex, Fitness, and Food in the Legacy of Degeneracy Theory, Graham Crackers, Kellogg's Corn Flakes, and American Health History (1985).*

32. McHugh, Paul

    a. Psychiatric Misadventures

    b. The mind has mountains.

33. Money, J. and A. Ehrhardt

    a. (1972). Man and Woman, Boy and Girl. Baltimore, John Hopkins University Press.

    b. (1952). *Hermaphroditism: An Inquiry into the Nature of a Human Paradox.* Thesis (Ph.D.), Harvard University.

    c. Money, John, and Patricia Tucker. (1975). *Sexual Signatures on Being a Man or a Woman.* Little Brown & Co: Money, John.

    d. (1986). *Lovemaps: Clinical Concepts of Sexual/Erotic Health and Pathology, Paraphilia, and Gender Transposition in Childhood, Adolescence, and Maturity.* New York: Irvington. Money, John.

e. (1988*) Gay, Straight, and In-Between: The Sexology of Erotic Orientation.* New York: Oxford University Press.

f. (1989*). Vandalized Lovemaps: Paraphilic Outcome of 7 Cases in Pediatric Sexology.* Prometheus Books

g. (1994). *Sex Errors of the Body and Related Syndromes: A Guide to Counseling Children, Adolescents, and Their Families* , 2nd ed. Baltimore: P.H. Brooks Publishing CompanyMoney, John.

h. (1995). *Gendermaps: Social Constructionism, Feminism, and Sexosophical History.* New York: Continuum.

i. Money, John, and Anke Ehrhardt. (1996). *Man & Woman, Boy & Girl: Gender Identity from Conception to Maturity.* Northvale, N.J.: Jason Aronson. Money, John.

j. (1999). *The Lovemap Guidebook: A Definitive Statement.*

34. Schmidt, E. (2001). UCLA geneticists identify cause of malformed genitalia, finding will improve sex assignments in ambiguous newborns, UCLA Press release 1 May.

35. Simpson, J. A. and E. S. C. Weiner, Eds. (1989). Oxford English Dictionary. Oxford, England, Clarendon Press.

36. Stoller, R. J.

    a. Sex and gender: on the Development of Masculinity and Femininity (1968)

    b. Splitting: a Case of Female Masculinity (1973),

    c. Observing the Erotic Imagination (1985)

    d. co-wrote Cognitive Science and Psychoanalysis (1988) with K.M. Colby

    e. (1968). Sex and gender: (1974)

37. Cohort Study.

    a. Long-Term Follow-Up of Transsexual Persons Undergoing Sex Reassignment Surgery in Sweden

38. Zucker, K. J. (1990).

    a. Treatment of Gender Identity Disorders in Children. Clinical Management of Gender Identity Disorders in Children and Adults. R. Blanchard and B. W. Steiner. Washington, D.C., American Psychiatric Press, Inc.

    b. Gender Identity Disorder in Children and Adolescents. Treatment of Psychiatric Disorders. G. O. Gabbard. Washington, D.C, American Psychiatric Association. 2094. Zucker, K. J. and S. J. Bradley

    c. (1995). Gender identity disorder and psychosexual problems in children and adolescents. New York, The Guilford Press. Zucker, K. J., S. J. Bradley, et al.

   d. 1992. "Gender Identity Disorder in
     Children." Annual Review of Sex Research

39. Wise TN, Meyer JK (1980).

40. The border area between transvestism and gender dysphoria: transvestic applicants for sex reassignment. Archives of Sexual Behavior . 1980 Aug;9

41. Lothstein LM

42. (1979). Psychological treatment of transsexualism and sexual identity disorders: some recent attempts. Archives of Sexual Behavior .
Wise TN, Dupkin C, Meyer JK (1981). Partners of distressed transvestites. American Journal of Psychiatry . 1981 Sep
Wise TN, Lucas J (1981). Pseudotranssexualism: iatrogenic gender dysphoria. Journal of Homosexuality . 1981 Spring;

43. Association (1987). Diagnostic and Statistical Manual of Mental Disorders (DSM III-IV-V).

22597151R00133

Made in the USA
Columbia, SC
29 July 2018